POLICY PAPERS

NUMBER 27

PALESTINIAN SELF-GOVERNMENT (AUTONOMY): ITS PAST AND ITS FUTURE

HARVEY SICHERMAN

THE WASHINGTON INSTITUTE FOR NEAR EAST POLICY
WASHINGTON, D.C.

Library of Congress Cataloging-in-Publication Data

Sicherman, Harvey.
    Palestinian Self-government (Autonomy): Its Past and Its
Future / Harvey Sicherman.
        p. cm. – (Policy papers ; no. 27)
        ISBN 0-944029-14-0 : $11.95
        1. Jewish-Arab relations—1973. 2. Palestinian Arabs—
Politics and government. 3. Autonomy. 4. Egypt.   Treaties, etc.
Israel, 1978 Sept. 17 (Framework for Peace in the Middle East)   5.
United States—Foreign relations—Middle East.   6.   Middle East—
Foreign relations—United States.   7.   United States—Foreign
relations—1977-1981.   8.   United States—Foreign relations—1981-1989.
I. Title. II. Series: Policy papers (Washington Institute for Near East
Policy) : no. 27.
    DS119.7.S38194   1991
    956—dc20   91-32273
                                                                CIP

Cover design by Jill Indyk

THE AUTHOR

Dr. Harvey Sicherman, a consultant on International Relations, wrote this study as a visiting fellow at The Washington Institute for Near East Policy. A former special assistant to Secretary of State Alexander M. Haig Jr., he also served as a consultant to Secretary of State George P. Shultz. Most recently, Dr. Sicherman was a member of the State Department's Policy Planning Staff under Secretary James A. Baker III. He is the author of numerous books and articles including *Changing the Balance of Risks: U.S. Policy Toward the Arab-Israeli Conflict* (The Washington Institute, 1988).

The opinions expressed in this Policy Paper are those of the author and should not be construed as representing those of The Washington Institute for Near East Policy, its Board of Trustees or its Board of Advisors.

CONTENTS

ACKNOWLEDGMENTS

Martin Indyk must take the blame for having put me on to this project, after lulling me with good food and drink.

A long list of the people touched by the autonomy negotiations who gave freely of their time and advice includes: Former Secretary of State Alexander M. Haig Jr., Ambassador Sol Linowitz, Ambassador Richard Fairbanks, Ambassador James Leonard, Ambassador Samuel W. Lewis, Sherwood Goldberg, M. Charles Hill, Alan J. Kreczko, William T. Kirby, Daniel Kurzer, Dan Haendel, Ruth Lapidoth, William Quandt and Elyakim Rubinstein. Of course, they are in no way responsible for errors of fact or interpretation, which I claim for my very own.

The Washington Institute as always proved a productive place to work, a place of smiling faces (yes, Dana and Carole) and kindly insistence that deadlines be met. Special thanks go to Lila Segal, Sharon Joffe, and Ellen Rice—all of whom qualified for hieroglyphics before the project concluded. Their talents at ferreting out the facts have made them more familiar with autonomy than I am sure they ever cared to be. And Yehudah Mirsky wielded his editor's pen like an anesthetic, so that I was barely conscious of the pain of excision.

Finally, thanks to my wife Barbara and my children, who need suffer no longer the embarrassment of unexpected mutterings, public and private, as thoughts congealed on this work.

PREFACE

Describing the changes of heart and mind which reordered the Middle East in the wake of the First World War, Albert Hourani, one of the great scholars of the modern Middle East has written: "Wars are catalysts, bringing to consciousness feelings hitherto inarticulate and creating expectations of change." The Gulf War of early 1991 bears the signs of having been such a catalyst. Having proved its assertiveness and strength, and having led a wide-ranging coalition into battle, the United States has, since the war's end, embarked on an energetic diplomatic effort, aimed at settling the long-standing conflict between the majority of the Arab states and Israel. The peace conference which Secretary of State James Baker has organized will grapple with a number of issues. One of the most contentious and significant will be the future of the Palestinians of Gaza and the West Bank.

We have been down this road before. When Egypt and Israel signed the historic Camp David Accords in 1978, they pledged to negotiate a workable future for the Palestinians, beginning with an interim period of self-government, or autonomy. This first, interim goal was never achieved, despite years of diplomatic effort, in large part because the Palestinians themselves chose not to take part in the discussions, a stance which thoughtful Palestinians may now regret. Today, as negotiations between Palestinians and Israelis hopefully get under way, the concept of autonomy is sure to be revived, and with it, a number of questions: What exactly is this "autonomy" or as it is now called, "self-government?" Where does the idea come from? What kinds of rights and responsibilities might it encompass? What are the chances of its success? And, finally, is it a good idea?

Fortunately, these questions need not be answered in a vacuum. The post-Camp David negotiations between Egypt and Israel, and the fits and starts of Mideast diplomacy in the 1980s, left behind a fascinating, if largely unexamined, record. Many of the questions sure to arise during the course of this latest round of peacemaking were discussed during earlier diplomatic rounds and looking at that record can help us understand autonomy's meaning, limits and possibilities.

There are few scholars better equipped to examine the meaning of Palestinian autonomy than Dr. Harvey Sicherman, a seasoned diplomatic historian and veteran of government, and a long-time associate of The Washington Institute. In anticipation of the Middle East peace conference he has scoured the written record of earlier autonomy negotiations, interviewed many of the participants and exhaustively thought through the meaning of that past experience and the message it bears for today. This exceptionally timely, judicious and gracefully written study is a fine example of the special contribution that scholarship can make to current policy debates.

Barbi Weinberg
President
October 1991

EXECUTIVE SUMMARY

On November 19, 1977, President Anwar Sadat of Egypt astounded the world when he visited Jerusalem to pursue peace talks directly with Israeli Prime Minister Menachem Begin. Addressing the Knesset the next day, Sadat insisted that a solution to the Arab-Israeli conflict include a Palestinian "right to statehood." Thus challenged, some six weeks later Begin unveiled Israel's response: "self rule" or "autonomy" for the Palestinian Arabs under Israeli military government.

After excruciating negotiations, a version of this idea of autonomy became part of the Camp David Accords signed by Egypt, Israel and the United States on September 17, 1978. Unlike the Egyptian-Israeli Peace Treaty, however, Camp David's "full autonomy"—a five-year transitional arrangement for a freely elected self-governing authority (sometimes referred to as an administrative council) for the inhabitants of the West Bank and Gaza—never came to life. The Palestinians (and Jordan) rejected the idea and, despite intensive negotiations, Egypt, Israel and the United States could not agree on all of its terms. Then, after three years of effort, Egypt suspended the talks in August of 1982 in response to Israel's invasion of Lebanon.

This grim record would seem at first of merely academic interest, another dead end in a conflict full of dead ends. But the Autonomy concept—that of an interim agreement in the West Bank and Gaza giving more government to Palestinians and less control to Israelis—did not perish. The 1980s showed that neither international pressure on behalf of the PLO nor the *intifadah* would force Israel to yield Judea, Samaria and the Gaza District (as it is known in Israel) or the West Bank and Gaza (as it is known to everyone else) to an Arab sovereignty in a single step—if ever. While the Palestinians and their allies have spent their time and energies pushing for statehood, the number of Israeli settlers in the territories (excluding Jerusalem) has steadily increased from 10,000 in 1980 to 100,000 today.

Meanwhile the Palestinian situation has also grown measurably worse. The hopes raised by the *intifadah*, the PLO's dialogue with the United States and then by Saddam Hussein have all been dashed. Even the demographic situation which for so long argued in favor of the Palestinians has been altered by the influx of great numbers of Soviet Jews into Israel. Clearly an independent Palestinian state seems further than ever from fruition, and a more realistic Palestinian (and Arab) approach may be underway. As Secretary of State James A. Baker III said after his flurry of trips in the spring of 1991, he had found "agreement that the negotiations between Israel and the Palestinians would proceed in phases, with talks on interim self-government preceding negotiations over the permanent status of the Occupied Territories."

Notably, of course, the current discussions of such an interim agreement do not include the words "autonomy" or "Camp David." For although the Palestinians and the Arabs may be well on their way toward accepting both the concept and the framework, they do not wish to encumber their journey with embarrassing historical baggage.

The way is marked nonetheless, with the signposts of irony. While to the dictionary autonomy means "self-government," to the Palestinians the word represents an Israeli attempt to limit their sovereignty. The Israelis for their part see "self-government" as a term fairly bursting with sovereignty and at Camp David insisted successfully that the Self-Governing Authority, as autonomy was to be known, be described parenthetically as an administrative council.

It may therefore be both more convenient and still quite accurate to describe the matter differently by calling the proposed regime "Palestinian Self-Government (Autonomy)." This expresses both the Palestinians' greatest hope for the concept's future and its necessary bloodline to the past, its roots in limited powers that respect Israeli aspirations and interests.

Throughout this essay these terms—self-government and autonomy—will be used interchangeably unless otherwise noted.

My main purpose, however, is not to preoccupy otherwise gainfully unemployed political philologists. Now that Self-Government (Autonomy) is once again of interest, two important questions must be answered: Will it solve the Palestinian problem, or at least put it on the road to solution? And how could the United States help to bring this about?

This essay hopes to answer such questions through a review of autonomy's past and an exploration of its potential as a form of self-government. Revisiting the past will surely not amuse the reader or titillate the diplomats; there is precious little entertainment in the record. It does, however, establish these points: (1) **Interim Agreements Are Not the Last Word:** Attempts to "guarantee" the end game through an interim agreement will make even the interim step impossible. Self-government (autonomy) does not assure Palestinian national independence nor does it guarantee Israeli sovereignty over the territory. (2) **The "Last Word" Will Still Intrude:** Notwithstanding autonomy's deliberate ambiguity, long-term consequences flow from different negotiating positions, and the fear of those consequences will intrude even as interim steps are discussed. (3) **Outside Help Will Be Needed:** Given the risks to be run by both sides on issues such as security, land, water, settlements and Jerusalem, outside help in reducing these risks and overcoming the obstacles will be necessary. The U.S. remains best suited to play the role of mediator, but other international support will also be needed both within the region and outside of it. (4) **The Deal Must Work On Its Own Terms:** Autonomy **can** facilitate state-to-state peace diplomacy (it did so for Egypt and Israel) **but only** if those states have decided to seek peace on sound bilateral foundations. Conversely, a larger peace process involving state-to-state negotiations can work to encourage an autonomy agreement, but it cannot be a substitute for an Israeli-Palestinian deal that works for both sides.

I then take these lessons and explore (1) the impact that subsequent peace plans—Reagan (1982), Peres-Hussein (1985), Shultz (1988), Shamir-Rabin (1989) and Baker (1989-90)—have had on the autonomy concept, and (2) the probable development of Palestinian Self-Government, should it occur, with special emphasis on America's role.

My general conclusion is this: If ever there was a time for Palestinian Self-Government (Autonomy), that time is now. Only on the much disputed ground between Israelis and Palestinian Arabs in the territories can there be found the strongest common interest in changing the status quo. Only through the transitional device of Palestinian Self-Government (Autonomy) can that change be most safely made to each party's advantage, without forcing them to yield what they will not yet yield; namely, their conflicting claims of sovereignty. And, ultimately, only through lasting improvement in Israeli-Palestinian relations can the decades-long strife in the Holy Land draw to a close.

U.S. policy, then, should focus on facilitating an agreement on Self-Government (Autonomy) by (1) using its good offices to recruit broader Arab and international support, (2) isolating those who would obstruct it, (3) helping the parties, which must include both recognized Palestinian representatives and, at some point, Jordan, to overcome the obstacles, (4) concentrating in particular on the land, water and security issues, the essence of any agreement on self-government, and (5) offering some guarantee of support for the result, whether political, economic, or military, as was done in every successful Arab-Israeli agreement thus far. The history of the Arab-Israeli conflict is a chronicle of missed opportunities. This latest chance to improve relations between those fated to live together is an opportunity that the parties—and the United States—should not miss again.

I ORIGINS OF AUTONOMY

WHAT WAS AUTONOMY AND HOW DID IT ORIGINATE?

The concept of Autonomy, or "Self-Rule for the Palestinian Arabs," was fathered by Menachem Begin, grandfathered by his great mentor Ze'ev Jabotinsky and midwifed into the Camp David Accords by Jimmy Carter with an assist from Anwar Sadat. Its conception, birth and subsequent history were very much a product of evolving views on how to settle the Arab-Israeli conflict, and especially the Palestinian dimension.

When Menachem Begin was unexpectedly elected to the Israeli premiership in May 1977, he was already uncomfortably aware of a dramatic change in U.S. policy on the Arab-Israeli conflict. After the 1967 war, Israel had come to control not only the territory of Mandatory Palestine up to the Jordan River, but also the Sinai Peninsula and the Golan Heights. United Nations Security Council Resolution 242, which formally ended hostilities, called for Israeli withdrawal "from occupied territories" and the establishment of peaceful, secure and recognized borders for all states [See Appendix I]. While the Arab governments and most members of the UN argued that Israel must withdraw to the pre-1967 lines, the U.S. position was that the extent of withdrawal was subject to negotiation while the principle of "territory for peace" applied to all fronts. Then, in the aftermath of the October 1973 war, Jordan's claim to the territories it had lost six years earlier was supplanted by the PLO's demand for an independent Palestinian state.

Israel's two major parties were opposed to total (or near total) withdrawal as a condition for peace and certainly opposed to a Palestinian state. Immediately after the 1967 War the then-Labour government had offered near-total withdrawal from Sinai and the Golan, and a two-thirds withdrawal from the West Bank—in return for peace and security.[1] But once this was rejected by the Arabs at the Khartoum Summit (August 1967), successive Labour governments in power until 1977 made clear that Israel would insist on substantial border changes on each front. Strategic settlements were planted in the Sinai, the Golan, the West Bank and Gaza. In the West Bank, known to Israelis by the biblical names of Judea and Samaria, almost all of those settlements were placed in the Jordan Valley, north and south of Jericho, clear of the major Arab population centers (Kiryat Arba and Kedumin were exceptions). Throughout these years, Israel invited the King of Jordan to a fresh territorial division that would give Israel buffer zones along the Jordan River.

The Likud bloc, headed by Menachem Begin, opposed any territorial compromise at all in Judea and Samaria. Likud hoped to incorporate the area as part of the historic Land of Israel. A much more aggressive Israeli settlement program in these territories was essential to Likud's program.

Until March of 1977, the United States officially advocated a Jordanian "option" for resolving the West Bank issue with border modifications more modest than Labour had in mind. Yet this position was steadily overtaken by Palestinian political developments. In 1974 at Rabat, the Arab states themselves had disqualified Jordan from representing the Palestinians, vesting this right instead in the Palestine Liberation Organization. For three years thereafter, the PLO ascended the ladder of growing international recognition and attained observer status at the UN. Simultaneously, the Arabs, the Soviets and their allies sought to isolate Israel and undermine its legitimacy, reaching a milestone in 1975 when the UN General Assembly resolved that Zionism was a form of racism.

---

[1] See Abba Eban, *Abba Eban: An Autobiography,* (New York: Random House, 1977), pp. 436-447: Israel sought peace treaties with Egypt and Syria "based on the former international boundaries with changes for Israel's security. . . . "

That same year Israel secured American pledges that the U.S. would neither recognize nor negotiate with the PLO unless the PLO recognized Israel and accepted Resolution 242. But this barrier did not prevent the newly elected U.S. President Jimmy Carter from declaring in March 1977 his support for a "Palestinian Homeland" as part of a comprehensive settlement of the Arab-Israeli conflict—a formula the Zionists regarded as a euphemism for statehood.[2] It was under these highly alarming circumstances that Begin took office, strongly opposed to both territorial compromise and a Palestinian state.

Despite predictions of imminent disaster from both sides, both Carter and Begin avoided a direct clash when the Israeli Prime Minister debuted in Washington in July of 1977. Begin sidestepped the American attempt to force him to declare that 242 required some Israeli withdrawal (if not total) on all fronts; he stated instead that his problem was not with the U.S., but with Israel's Arab neighbors. Once the Arabs stepped forward to negotiate, these matters could be worked out. Following Begin's visit, the U.S. redoubled its efforts throughout that summer to reconvene an international conference—including Palestinians—to make a comprehensive settlement.

On August 8, 1977, Carter again aroused Israeli apprehensions by declaring that if the PLO accepted 242, the U.S. would open discussions for the purpose of making it a partner to a negotiation. Begin was already convinced that Israel needed a "Palestinian proposal," something that offered a change in the status quo without violating his ideological principles. He told visiting Secretary of State Cyrus Vance on August 10 that Israel would give "our Arab neighbors in Judea, Samaria and Gaza full cultural autonomy" and a choice of Israeli citizenship.[3]

---

[2]The Balfour Declaration of 1917 had pledged to facilitate a "home in Palestine" for the Jewish people, which eventually became the state of Israel.

[3]William Quandt, *Camp David: Peacemaking and Politics*, (Washington: Brookings, 1986), p. 92.

"TO THE ENDS OF THE EARTH"

Vance was preoccupied with the diplomacy that led to Syrian and PLO vetoes over a conference, and the joint U.S.-Soviet communique of October 1, 1977 which appeared to grant the USSR a decisive role in the peacemaking. Fearful that American policy was putting the entire process into the hands of his enemies, Sadat instead pursued direct contacts with Israel. Secret meetings, including one in Morocco between Israeli Foreign Minister Moshe Dayan and Hassan Tuhami, Sadat's agent, convinced Sadat that the Likud Government would trade Sinai for peace. He thereupon embarked on his self-declared journey "to the ends of the earth" for peace that brought him to Jerusalem on November 19, 1977—to everyone's surprise, especially Washington's.[4]

Sadat made clear from the outset that he had not gone to Jerusalem to sign less than a comprehensive peace agreement with Israel. He also indicated, however, that Egypt would not do the work of the other Arab states, or the Palestinians, for them. After all, Sadat's initiative was intended to free Egypt of the vetoes of the others who could block peace but who would rely on Egypt's willingness to shed its blood in the event of war. Instead he offered Begin a concept of "full peace": a resumption of Arab sovereignty on every front Israel had captured in 1967, but with peace and security for Israel. On the West Bank that meant a "self determination" that might unite the Palestinian population with Jordan. As for Gaza, there Egypt could play a special role.

Begin could not accept these ideas, and both sides treated the initial exchange as only the beginning of negotiations. The two leaders decided to continue their dialogue at humbler diplomatic levels, in preparation for a summit at the Suez Canal port of Ismailia on December 25, 1977, when Begin would respond with his own proposals. On December 2, Dayan met Tuhami again, hoping to duplicate the success of his earlier meeting, but this time on the Palestinian issue he found the Egyptian unbending. Dayan nonetheless gave Tuhami a

---

[4]For a fuller account of this sequence see Martin Indyk, *"To the Ends of the Earth:" Sadat's Jerusalem Initiative,* (Cambridge, Massachusetts: Harvard Center for Middle Eastern Studies, 1984).

preview of what Begin intended to bring to Sadat on the Palestinian issue.[5]

The Carter Administration, which had cultivated a close relationship with Sadat, was thoroughly nonplussed by this sudden explosion of bilateral activity. After the breakthrough, the President and his men had decided to await events. To their surprise, it was Begin and not Sadat who showed up first to solicit America's help. Specifically, the Israeli Prime Minister wanted American support for his new plan of Palestinian autonomy.

Sadat's dramatic gesture had put enormous pressure on Israel to negotiate, and Begin had been thinking big—at least in his own terms. After Sadat's visit, Begin had dictated his plan in secret to his personal aide Yehiel Kadishai. It was an elaboration with some crucial changes of a concept developed by Begin's personal hero and the Likud's ideological mentor, the controversial early Zionist leader Ze'ev Jabotinsky.

"SELF-RULE OF THE NATIONAL MINORITY"

Begin's autonomy proposal could not have been unfamiliar to the older hands in his own party. In fact, he had taken one side of a long-running argument that ran to the earliest period of Zionist political history. Begin's scheme invoked the ideas of none other than his party's mentor, Ze'ev Jabotinsky, who, like other early Zionist theoreticians, wrestled with the problems posed by two turn-of-the-century national minorities: the Jews, as they were then domiciled throughout the multinational empires of Europe; and the Arabs of Palestine, already opposed to burgeoning Zionist settlement.

Jabotinsky believed that nationalism was defined by personal preference—the individual's sense of national identity—rather than by race, place of residence or even language. Every individual had rights, and these rights, so Jabotinsky thought, could be accommodated by a national majority in a manner that respected both national sovereignty and minority dignity. This he called "personal autonomy." Jabotinsky had explored the personal autonomy concept in a

---

[5]See Moshe Dayan, *Breakthrough*, (New York: Alfred Knopf, 1981), pp. 93-7.

thesis that earned him a law degree in 1912, entitled *Self-Rule of the National Minority*.[6]

Whatever his later reputation, Jabotinsky was among the very few early Zionists who concluded that the Arabs living in the land of Israel were in fact a nation with legitimate claims that could never be reconciled with Zionism. Because he reasoned that the Jewish historical and national claim to the land was superior, he concluded that the Arabs would have to be content with minority self-rule: "to grant the Arab minority in Eretz Israel every possible right that the Jews claimed for themselves, but had never achieved in other countries."[7]

There was another competing idea in the 1920s and the 1930s, especially after the Peel Commission had concluded in 1937 that partition was the best way to resolve the Arab-Jewish conflict: Arab populations who were unwilling to live as a minority in the Jewish state, would be "transferred" to the Arab state or states. This idea was more easily accepted because many Zionists did not view the Palestinian Arabs as a separate nation, but as a branch of an Arab nation already enjoying many states—including Transjordan, severed from the Palestinian Mandate by the British to accommodate their World War I Hashemite Arab allies from the Arabian peninsula.[8] Ultimately, by this reasoning, there might be a repeat of the Turkish-Greek settlement of 1923, which finally resolved one of the more murderous ethnic problems of modern times.[9]

---

[6] See Ze'ev Jabotinsky, "Self-Rule of the National Minority," *Writings*, (Jerusalem: Book Publishing Company *[Hebrew]*, 1950).

[7] Quoted in Yaacov Shavit, *Jabotinsky and the Revisionist Movement 1925-1948*, (London: Frank Cass Ltd., 1988), p. 258.

[8] The occasionally entertaining circumstances surrounding the establishment of the then-Amir (later King) Abdullah in Transjordan are related in Sir Alec Kirkbride, *A Crackle of Thorns: Experiences in the Middle East*, (London: John Murray, 1956).

[9] After Israel was established, most of the Jewish communities in the Arab countries moved in fear of their lives to the new State; many Israelis thus claimed that this population exchange had indeed taken place, the Jews of Arabia having traded places with the Arabs of Palestine.

Although he thought voluntary, albeit encouraged, transfer was desirable, Jabotinsky rejected "forced transfer" as both immoral and impractical. He settled on the Self-Rule concept as the best solution. All would enjoy common citizenship in the Zionist polity, but the Arabs would be free to cultivate Home Rule and their unique cultural and religious institutions. And it was this concept, hallowed by Jabotinsky's authority, that Begin chose to elaborate.[10]

Begin devised a plan that he originally described as "Home-Rule." The Likud leader's proposal, however, also contained a major departure from Jabotinsky. Instead of Jabotinsky's Self-Government under Israeli sovereignty, Begin decided to leave the question of sovereignty open,[11] offering the residents instead a choice of Israeli or Jordanian citizenship. Checking with Aharon Barak, his Attorney General, who had been asked to develop the plan's detail, the legally-minded Begin discovered that this alteration raised an important problem. What would be the source of legal authority for the powers granted the Home-Rule? If it were the Israeli Military Government, that would require its retention in some form, yet Begin desired to dispense with the Military Government, symbol of an abnormal situation.[12]

Aside from its ideological merits, self-government/ autonomy/Home-Rule for the Palestinians had another advantage. Demographically, a decision by the Arabs in the territories to adopt Israeli citizenship en masse could trigger a political disaster; the Arabs might soon hold the swing vote.

---

[10]Writing in the Hebrew newspaper *Ha'aretz* on Feb. 4, 1988, the veteran Land Of Israel Movement activist Israel Eldad quoted Begin as saying as early as 1975: "Sinai is not Eretz Yisrael and we shall give the Arabs autonomy." Autonomy, Begin explained, was Jabotinsky's position at the 1906 Zionist Helsinki Conference which had debated the question of how to deal with local Arab opposition to Zionism. Quoted in Ehud Sprinzak, *The Ascendance of Israel's Radical Right,* (New York: Oxford University Press, 1991), p. 331, n. 7. See also Ze'ev B. Begin, "A Vision for Israel at Peace," *Foreign Affairs,* Fall 1991, p. 33. Begin, the Prime Minister's son, confirms the origin of autonomy in Jabotinsky's writings.

[11]See Begin, *Foreign Affairs,* p.33: ". . . Arab autonomy is not now conceived as under Israeli sovereignty. This was a far reaching leap in Likud thinking and is a significant concession on its part."

[12]See Quandt, *op. cit.,* p. 155 for an account of this background.

But if they were granted a local self-government distinct from national sovereignty and a choice of Jordanian citizenship, this dire prospect could be avoided. In short, personal autonomy for the Arabs of the West Bank and Gaza, to Begin's mind, recognized their just minority rights without running the international or domestic political risks of incorporating a restive Palestinian population into the Israeli polity.

BEGIN GOES TO WASHINGTON

When the Israeli Prime Minister arrived in Washington on December 16, he found the Carter Administration wary that his surprise visit was intended to outflank Sadat. And Begin did indeed solicit support for Home-Rule, stressing these key points: 1) sovereignty claims would be set aside or left open; 2) there would be free elections for an Arab "Administrative Council" with limited powers; 3) Israel would retain responsibility for security, and 4) there would be elements of reciprocity between Israel and the Council regarding issues such as land purchases, settlement, immigration and water development. Admitting that the source of authority was a sticky legal problem, Begin attributed it nonetheless to the Israeli Military Government as the ultimate authority. This arrangement, Begin suggested, would be permanent.

Vance, Brzezinski, Carter and their aides were dubious about the proposed "Home-Rule" because, in their view, it could be no substitute for Israeli withdrawal and the assumption of an Arab sovereignty over the areas, a final outcome to which they were committed by their reading of 242.[13] They urged Begin to present it as a transitional or interim scheme, not a permanent solution, a position he had no difficulty in accepting because his plan contained a "review" option after five years—a year beyond the maximum time an Israeli parliament could serve before new elections were required. If autonomy was indeed merely transitional, then the Americans saw Begin's proposals as a "step forward."[14]

---

[13]See Cyrus Vance, *Hard Choices: Critical Years in America's Foreign Policy*, (New York: Simon and Schuster, 1983), p. 54. Also pp. 196-98.

[14]Quandt, *op. cit.*, p. 157. In the first misunderstanding between the two leaders, Begin later claimed that Carter had agreed that the Israeli

NSC Advisor Zbigniew Brzezinski thought Begin's idea had possibilities, but, interestingly, his suggested improvements would have turned Autonomy into a kind of "Israeli Mandate" for a Palestinian state. (Brzezinski himself had advocated a demilitarized Palestinian state several years earlier.) The military government, he argued, should be replaced by an authority with other participatory powers, such as Jordan or the UN. A specifically UN presence would help to reinforce the idea that the transition scheme was based on 242, and a Palestinian "assembly" could meet in East Jerusalem to indicate that that area was part of the transition.[15] (Begin's plan had placed the seat of "self-rule" in Bethlehem.)

Begin left Washington persuaded of Carter's initial support for a transitional scheme, and he tried out the idea on British Prime Minister Callaghan in London with similar results. Containing 26 points, the plan was then retitled, at Dayan's urging, as "Self-Rule for Palestinian Arabs, Residents of Judea, Samaria and the Gaza District which will be Instituted upon the Establishment of Peace." [See Appendix III]

The Israeli Foreign Minister, who had also influenced Begin to be more specific about Jordan's role, had his own ideas on autonomy. These were similar to Begin's insofar as giving local government to the Palestinians, but predicated on a desire 1) to hold the areas through Jewish settlement, economic ties and joint infrastructure, while separating them politically from Israel so as to retain the Jewish character of the state; 2) to give the Arabs "functional" responsibility for local politics and administration; and 3) to make Jordan a political focus for the Palestinians who could not find such an outlet in Israel.

"Functional co-existence," in Dayan's view, could best be embodied politically by autonomy or self-rule for the Arabs.

---

autonomy proposal was a "fair basis for negotiation." Carter thought this was exaggerated, especially because in Carter's opinion, the autonomy proposal Begin put to Sadat was "attenuated substantially." See Jimmy Carter, *Keeping Faith: Memoirs of a President*, (New York: Bantam, 1982), p. 300. Quandt disagrees with Carter, arguing that the proposals were substantially the same. See Quandt, *op. cit.*, p. 158.

[15]Zbigniew Brzezinski, *Power and Principle*, (New York: Farrar, Strauss, Giroux, 1983), pp. 118-19.

He was convinced that continued Israeli military rule or the extension of Israeli law and administration over an innately hostile population would produce disaster.[16] Ezer Weizman, then Begin's Defense Minister, would later crystallize this idea even further: "They [the Palestinians] can have their own authorities and run their own affairs as they see fit—just as long as they do not threaten us."[17]

---

[16]See Dayan, *op. cit.*, pp. 303-04 on this theme.

[17]Ezer Weizman, *Battle for Peace*, (New York: Bantam, 1981), p. 388.

II "A LITTLE AIR": AUTONOMY AND CAMP DAVID

Begin's autonomy plan had extricated the Prime Minister from the straitjacket of the Likud's territorial claim by deferring the application of the claim itself. This was painful but not politically fatal. But the secret preparation of the plan and Begin's penchant for using grandiose adjectives in describing it aroused apprehension across party lines. The charge stuck that it would create the institutional foundation of a Palestinian state,[1] leading the Prime Minister to be hypersensitive about anything that suggested "sovereign" powers or symbols. Nonetheless, autonomy did establish a singular Israeli benchmark: a Begin/Likud-sponsored change in the status quo that did not increase, and in fact would decrease, both Israel's military presence and its administrative control.

Autonomy's international debut, however, played to less than rave reviews. Travelling to Ismailia on December 25, 1977, Begin unveiled his plan to Sadat, who had already heard the general provisions of the plan from both Tuhami and Carter. The atmosphere, devoid of any symbolic welcome for the Israelis, was made further surreal when Sadat began the

---

[1]See United States Foreign Broadcast Information Service (FBIS) December 28, 29, 30, 1977 for accounts of the Knesset (parliamentary) debate. Shimon Peres, the leading spokesman for the Labour opposition, declared that self-government could never be confined only to the administrative level.

meeting by swearing in his new Foreign Minister (his predecessor had resigned in protest). Begin rose (or sank) to the occasion. As Ezer Weizman recounted it, Begin offered a long presentation on a peace treaty with Egypt and then, with hardly a pause, treated a crowded, overheated room of officials to an equally detailed reading of his 26 point autonomy proposal, concluding his remarks by invoking the international legal authorities of his law studies in pre-war Poland, Lauterpacht and Oppenheim. "Sadat clapped his hands, and a waiter appeared. 'Iftach al Shubach, Open the window,' the President commanded. A little air entered the smoke-filled chamber."[2]

Yet the "little air" let in by the autonomy plan was enough to inflate the tires of the peace process. It would eventually enable Sadat and the Americans to justify a separate peace as not separate at all. It allowed Begin to offer something for the Palestinians without fatally impairing his political support. In fact, it did everything expected of it except provide autonomy for the Palestinians, not least because they violently rejected the concept.

AUTONOMY MAKES THE DEAL

After Ismailia, the Egyptian-Israeli direct negotiations reached a complete impasse. The full story of how the United States intervened to aid the talks, eventually culminating in the extraordinary sessions at Camp David, need not be retold here. Suffice it to say that the fortunes of Begin's autonomy proposals were affected by three events. First, Carter's trip to Aswan to confer with Sadat in January 1978, produced a crucial compromise on Egypt's insistence that Israel recognize Palestinian self-determination. Israel eventually came to accept the Carter formula, the Palestinian right "to participate in the determination of their own future" which was written into the Camp David Accords. Second, at a meeting in Leeds Castle between the Foreign Ministers of Egypt and Israel in June 1978, Dayan was able to fashion agreement on a number of concepts: a five year duration for autonomy, as a transitional arrangement; a "withdrawal" of the Israeli Military Government; elections for a Palestinian self-government;

---

[2]Ezer Weizman, *Battle for Peace*, (New York: Bantam, 1981), p. 132.

retention by Israel of security rights; and a special role for Jordan in the arrangement, apart from an Israeli-Jordanian negotiation over a separate peace treaty. Third, on August 13, 1978 in the preliminary discussions before Camp David, the U.S. team decided that a refashioned autonomy was the only way to facilitate an overall Egyptian-Israeli agreement.

It is worth quoting in full the words of William Quandt, the NSC staff member who recorded the U.S. position:

> The key idea was to refashion Begin's autonomy plan into a proposal that would offer the Palestinians a serious measure of self-government. The proposal would include a clear commitment to a second phase of negotiations toward the end of the transitional period to resolve the questions of borders, sovereignty and Palestinian rights in accordance with UN resolution 242—territory for peace—and Carter's promise at Aswan that Palestinians should have the right to participate in determining their own future.[3]

A MISTY PENUMBRA

It is illuminating to compare these points with the documents finally signed at Camp David on September 17, 1978 and with Begin's original 26 point presentation to the Knesset on December 28, 1977:

• Begin's plan had originally called for "administrative autonomy" to be run by an eleven-member "Administrative Council" with its seat in Bethlehem. The Camp David Accords call for "full autonomy" to be run by a "Self-Governing Authority (Administrative Council)", whose location and size are unspecified.

• Begin's plan urged that claims to sovereignty be left open "for the sake of peace," while Camp David stipulated two stages: autonomy first and then negotiations on the final status of the territories beginning no later than the third year of the five year autonomy.

• Begin's plan abolished the military "administration" but not the military government; Camp David "withdraws" the military government and it is "replaced."

---

[3]William Quandt, *Camp David: Peacemaking and Politics*, (Washington: Brookings, 1986), pp. 212-213.

• Begin's plan would have Israel devolve autonomy on the Palestinians, while in Camp David a complex negotiation involving Israel, Egypt, Jordan, the Palestinians and the U.S. would establish the autonomy and a continuing committee would also be created to supervise it, among other duties.

• Begin's plan offered the residents of the West Bank and Gaza a choice of Israeli or Jordanian citizenship and the right to vote for the Knesset or the Jordanian Parliament, and a joint Israeli-Jordanian Committee to harmonize legislation with the Palestinian Administrative council that was to be created. None of this "confederal overture" appears in Camp David, thus giving the inhabitants of the Self-Governing Authority a status more independent of both Israel and Jordan.

• Begin's plan put security and public order among Israeli responsibilities. Camp David calls for a "strong local police force" with possible Jordanian participation, and withdrawal of Israeli security forces to specified locations.

• Begin's plan embraced an "open borders" concept; allowing for an Israeli right to purchase land and settle in the areas and a Palestinian right to purchase land and settle in Israel—if the Palestinian purchaser is an Israeli citizen. Again, none of this appeared in Camp David, and the settlements issue, as we shall see, continued to bedevil the proceedings.

• Finally, the Begin plan provided for a joint Israel-Jordan-Palestinian Administrative Council Committee to decide unanimously on "norms of immigration" for Arab refugees who wished to return. Camp David added Egypt and gave to a "continuing committee" the task of agreeing "on the modalities of admission of persons displaced from the West Bank and Gaza in 1967, together with necessary measures to prevent disruption and disorder."

The final Camp David provisions also added a lengthy exposition of how the Palestinians would at each stage participate "in the determination of their own future" and the achievement of their "legitimate rights": as part of the delegations negotiating the autonomy; through the elections of a self-governing authority; and through negotiating the final status. These provisions clearly reflect the impact of the American (and Egyptian) desire to turn Begin's autonomy into a transitional corridor leading to an Arab sovereignty. The Camp David Accords themselves, of course, do not spell that out, taking refuge instead in a "creative ambiguity." What happened immediately afterwards, however, indicated that none of the would-be peacemakers could leave this ambiguity alone.

Later, when Ambassador Sol Linowitz, Carter's second Special Negotiator, read through the President's personal notes on the Camp David Accords he was struck by the complexity of it all, and also by the myriad possibilities for misunderstanding.[4] An Israeli law professor took it further, concluding that "this misty penumbra of formulational ambiguity was created deliberately."[5] And in fact there is plenty of evidence from the recollections of the participants that rather than stall the proceedings over clarifications to the autonomy proposal, Carter, Sadat and Begin preferred to concentrate on Israeli military withdrawal from Sinai, the fate of Israeli settlements in the Sinai, security provisions in the south, and the extent of Egyptian-Israeli normalization.[6]

The conclusion of the Accords [See Appendix IV], after so many days of sometimes desperate negotiation, did not inspire an immediate feeling of triumph. Instead, there was a sense of foreboding and of work yet to be done.[7] This malaise dissipated somewhat in the public ceremony following the agreement, but even that grand occasion could not disguise the serious troubles ahead. Carter, in particular, had taken upon himself to act as a "full partner" and also to bring Saudi Arabia and Jordan into the negotiations. But on September 19, only two days after the Accords were signed, the Saudis said that Camp David "cannot be regarded as an acceptable final formula for peace." And this was not the only problem. The President and his men were also still determined to rectify any Israeli backsliding on ultimate satisfaction of minimal Palestinian

---

[4]Personal interview with Ambassador Linowitz.

[5]Amos Shapira in Yoram Dinstein, ed., *Models of Autonomy*, (New Brunswick: Transaction Books, 1981), p. 285.

[6]See Quandt's summary after ten days of negotiation and Carter's choices, *op. cit.*, pp. 235-36. Also p. 244 on the decision to "fuzz over the issue" of UNSC 242's application to the final status negotiations over the West Bank and Gaza.

[7]Quandt, *op. cit.*, pp. 253-54.

interests as they defined them. In other words, as Vance said of Begin's original autonomy presentation, it could not become a substitute for necessary Israeli withdrawal.[8]

As it turned out, both the U.S. and Israel hastened to clarify the misty penumbra, with disastrous results for the inaugural stage of the autonomy negotiations.

THE PEACEMAKERS FIGHT

A critical diplomatic weakness in the Camp David Accords was their incompleteness. In essence, Sadat and Begin were not taking home a peace treaty or an autonomy agreement, but only frameworks for reaching them. They, and Carter as well, would have to defend the not-yet-finished arrangements while simultaneously negotiating to finish them. In short, the Accords signalled to the opposition what might be coming but had not yet arrived.

Begin stood to be the biggest winner if he could secure real peace with Egypt without yielding the West Bank, and this eventuality was implicit in Sadat's own approach of not allowing the Palestinian issue to stymie Egypt's pursuit of her vital interests. But Begin had not reached his goal yet, and Carter was determined to show that the U.S. would not endorse anything less than a comprehensive peace. Otherwise, America's ability to attract others to the deal would be fatally impaired. Finally, Sadat had thrown himself into the arms of both Carter and Begin, reasoning that both had every interest in making him a winner.

Frederick the Great once observed that while Austrian Empress Maria Theresa had opposed the partition of Poland on moral grounds, when Prussia and Russia decided to go ahead with it anyhow, "she wept but she took." There was something of this sentiment in the American approach to the Camp David Accords. Carter "wept and took" the Accords while almost immediately thereafter trying to portray autonomy as a corridor to Arab sovereignty. Begin's "weeping" began when he discovered that, Jabotinsky notwithstanding, the autonomy proposal divided his party and forced him to rely on the Labour

---

[8]Cyrus Vance, *Hard Choices: Critical Years in America's Foreign Policy*, (New York: Simon and Schuster, 1983), pp. 196-98.

opposition to get the Camp David Accords through the Knesset. (Among prominent members of the Likud, Moshe Arens voted against while Yitzhak Shamir as speaker of the Knesset abstained, after making his opposition clear). Or as one Israeli wit put it, Begin offered up the Camp David autonomy before Jabotinsky's portrait and the portrait said, "What have you done, my son?"

Accused by his critics of preparing the way for a Palestinian state even before securing a peace with Egypt, Begin quickly reverted to his original autonomy ideas. The Americans helped speed the way through three controversial episodes: the Carter-Begin argument over settlements; the Saunders Mission; and above all, the written answers provided to a series of questions posed by Jordan's King Hussein.

The ink on the Camp David Accords was barely dry when President Carter and Prime Minister Begin fell into a hot controversy over "who said what" on the ever-touchy issue of Israeli settlements. Carter believed that he had extracted from Begin a settlements freeze for the duration of the autonomy negotiations. Begin asserted that all he had agreed to was a freeze for the three months the parties had stipulated for achieving a peace treaty (and for that matter, completing the autonomy negotiations as well). This very public quarrel embarrassed Carter and Begin at the very moment both sides were trying to "sell" the deal to skeptical audiences—Carter to the Arabs and Begin to his own party.[9]

Assistant Secretary of State Harold Saunders was dispatched to the area to preach Camp David's virtues to the Arabs and in particular to the Palestinians of the West Bank and Gaza. They, along with the "outside" PLO leadership, had been quick to react. Arafat warned that anyone supporting Sadat would "pay a high price" and later described autonomy as "no more than managing the sewers."[10] On September 18, 1978, the PLO

---

[9]See Quandt, *op. cit.*, pp. 248-50. He concludes that Begin originally meant three months tied to successful resolution of the autonomy talks but later tied it to the peace treaty. Dayan, on September 19, two days after the quarrel began, noted that Israel had in any case no plans to build any settlements for the next 90 days.

[10]For Arafat's comments see *Al Sharq' al-Awsat*, October 25, 1978 and May 25, 1979.

Executive Committee announced its "total rejection" of the
Accords. On October 1, 1978, one hundred leading Palestinians
from the Occupied Territories had publicly declared autonomy
to be "an open plot" against Palestinian rights, especially that of
self-determination."[11] Apparently attempting to counter the
argument that autonomy foreclosed Arab sovereignty,
Saunders was quoted in the Hebrew press as saying that the
areas "should return to Arab sovereignty"; even if not
accurately quoted, his efforts further angered the Israeli
government.[12] Whatever he said, however, paled by
comparison with the detailed positions provided by the Carter
Administration to the King of Jordan in October.

On September 19, Jordan had reiterated the "principles"
that would "govern its attitude" toward the Accords but offered
to withhold final judgement until a more intensive "appraisal"
could be made. This took the form of a Royal Questionnaire
addressed to Washington.

The Carter administration hoped that precise answers to the
King's questions about autonomy would elicit his support.
Among the more noteworthy American clarifications were: 1)
The "source of authority" would be the international
agreement itself and the "continuing committee" of Egypt,
Israel and Jordan as the Camp David Accords established. 2)
The Palestinian delegates on the Egyptian and Jordanian
negotiating teams could include "other Palestinians as
mutually agreed" (the Camp David Accords formula), who
must accept UN Security Council Resolution 242 and be
prepared to live in peace with Israel (a position which excluded
the PLO). 3) While the self-governing authority covered the
West Bank and Gaza, it was "not realistic to expect that the full
scope of the Self-Governing Authority can be extended to East
Jerusalem during the transitional period." Nonetheless,
Palestinians of East Jerusalem who are not Israeli citizens
should "participate in the elections to constitute the self-
governing authority and in the work of the self-governing
authority itself." 4) The Israeli settlers and settlements
although not mentioned in the Camp David framework, "will

---

[11] See also the political critique by Faisal Husseini in *Shu'un Filastiniya* No.
84 (Nov. 1978) concluding that "Sadat had sold the cause of Palestine."

[12] *Ha'aretz*, October 26, 1978.

have to be dealt with in the course of those negotiations" (both for transitional and final status). 5) Aside from reasserting its own interpretation of 242 (land for peace on all fronts) the U.S. also pledged to be "a full partner" in the negotiations, with President Carter taking "an active personal part".

Finally, the Administration described its own concept of a transitional period: "We see the transitional period as essential to build confidence, gain momentum and bring about the changes in attitude that can assure a final settlement which realizes the legitimate rights of the Palestinian people while assuring the security of Israel and of the other parties."[13]

These developments reinforced Begin's difficulties with his own party and even with the Labour opposition.[14] The sum total of America's actions definitely suggested that autonomy was a corridor leading to a reassertion of Arab sovereignty. The Prime Minister, who was having enough difficulty securing the Peace Treaty itself, had never conceived autonomy to be anything of the sort. As the Americans attempted to expand its meaning, Begin was trying to contract it. By and large, Sadat stood aside from this quarrel, which he viewed as American business with Israel.

At the end of October, the Israeli Cabinet decided to "strengthen" existing settlements, which was also the best way for Begin to strengthen the Likud coalition and rebuke the Americans. A committee chaired by the Director-General of Begin's office, Eliyahu Ben-Elissar, was established to create Israel's "detailed" plan—a rebuff to the answers provided by the U.S. to the King of Jordan. Its report, never published, was reported to be a restatement of Begin's original intent: the source of authority was to be the military government; autonomy meant autonomy of the person—the "inhabitants"— not the land; land and water resources were to be controlled by Israel, although water would be administered by a "joint

---

[13]All of the quotes are from Quandt's appendix H, *op. cit.*, pp. 388-96. His source is a copy made available by the government of Jordan, minus Carter's signature, the original being classified.

[14]Itamar Rabinovich, "The Autonomy Plan," *Middle East Contemporary Survey*, Volume III: 1978-79, (New York: Holmes and Meier, 1979), p. 170.

authority"; new settlements were most emphatically permitted.[15]

None of this was attractive to the Palestinians or the Jordanians, who continued to reject Camp David. The U.S. and Israel fought over autonomy just as the essential details of the Egyptian-Israeli treaty were being worked out. That treaty had its own complications, taking five months and Carter's personal intervention to conclude. Finally, when push came to shove on the treaty, all three partners decided to put aside the autonomy problem for another day—the basic decision they had made at Camp David, that they would reaffirm at the Peace Treaty signing and that they would reaffirm once more three years later when the moment arrived for the final Israeli withdrawal from Sinai.

Thus, on March 26, 1979, Begin and Sadat wrote a letter to Carter agreeing to begin autonomy negotiations within a month of the Peace Treaty's ratification. The letter itself, the product of excruciating negotiations, repeated the essentials of the Camp David framework, renewed an invitation to Jordan to participate and then added these provisions: 1) Egypt and Israel would negotiate an agreement even if Jordan did not participate; 2) the goal of these "continuous", "good faith" negotiations should be agreement within one year "so that elections will be held as expeditiously as possible . . . ;" 3) the United States would participate "fully in all stages of negotiations."[16] [See Appendix V]

---

[15]*Ibid*, p. 171.

[16]According to one participant, Egypt and the U.S. raised the issue of political "linkage" for the first time during the discussions preceding agreement on the letter. "Linkage" meant that if there should be no resolution of the autonomy issue, then Egyptian-Israeli relations could suffer. The Israelis thought they had settled this at Camp David, i.e., that the Peace Treaty stood by itself.

III THE "GOOD FAITH" NEGOTIATIONS: 1979-1980

True to their word, one month after their Peace Treaty, the Egyptians and Israelis, with their American partner, began to negotiate the meaning of the Self-Governing Authority (Administrative Council) as ordained by the Camp David Accords. They continued to do so, off and on, for three years. During that time, only Begin remained continuously in office; Sadat was murdered and succeeded by his Vice President Hosni Mubarak while Carter lost the 1980 election to Ronald Reagan. Three American "Personal Representatives," or Special Negotiators, tried their hand with varying success although there was considerable continuity at the working level amongst all of the teams.

The negotiations themselves may be divided into two stages. Stage I, 1979-80, began badly when the Americans tried to attract PLO support, but finished better once the second Special Negotiator, Sol Linowitz, concentrated on bringing Israel and Egypt to agreement on functional issues. Stage II, 1981-82, started late because Sadat refused to resume negotiations until after the Israeli election of June 1981. Begin and Sadat's joint determination in August 1981 to finish the negotiations by year's end engendered some progress but Sadat's murder two months later threw Egyptian resolve in doubt. By January 1982, U.S. Secretary of State Haig knew that neither Egypt nor Israel wanted the autonomy negotiations to impede the final Israeli withdrawal from Sinai.

It was then left to the third Special Negotiator, Richard Fairbanks, to isolate the underlying divisions between the parties and to prepare so-called bridging proposals. American plans to run a kind of Camp David II, however, fell victim to the Lebanon war and on August 16, 1982, Egypt suspended the negotiations pending an Israeli withdrawal from Lebanon and a "new concept." The U.S. proposals reappeared in part through the talking points that accompanied the Reagan Plan of September 1, 1982. Even though Autonomy was invoked as the subject of negotiations, that Plan shifted the focus decisively to the Jordan option and autonomy was relegated to the archives until the late 1980s when the entire concept was revived.

Throughout, several important political tendencies were to be observed among all the parties.

(1) *Different Concepts:* Egypt tried to dress the self-governing authority in the swaddling clothes of Palestinian sovereignty; Israel in the tightly fitted coat of a purely administrative autonomy, and the U.S. as a seasonal suit, to be worn temporarily and in all probability, to be succeeded by the mantle of an Arab sovereignty (Palestinian-Jordanian) for most of the territories.

2) *The Empty Chairs:* In the absence of the Palestinians or the Jordanians, neither Egypt nor Israel were inclined to reach "final" agreements. The Egyptians did not feel able to yield what they felt were the rights of those not present while the Israelis for their part had no reason to settle on a position that might require further change when (and if) the missing parties joined a negotiation. The United States was tempted to somehow "associate" the PLO or Jordan with the talks to supply missing links; these attempts usually served to drive the Egyptians and the Israelis apart.

(3) *Disturbing Linkage:* Although the autonomy provisions and the Egyptian-Israeli treaty were part of a comprehensive framework, each held independent legal validity. Beginning with the negotiations over the Sadat-Begin letter and throughout 1980-81, however, the U.S. and Egypt argued that the lack of agreement on autonomy would harm Egyptian-Israeli relations. Then, Israel's pressure for agreement on autonomy, as the date for Sinai withdrawal approached, led Egypt and the U.S. to fear that lack of agreement might impede the withdrawal itself. In both instances, as in every other crisis of the negotiations, all parties resolved on the primacy of the Egypt-Israel Peace Treaty, leaving autonomy for another day.

In other words, once the Treaty was done, autonomy, which had been a deal maker, did not become a deal breaker.

STUMBLE AND RECOVERY

Carter's pledge to remain closely and personally involved as a full partner soon took unique form. The President could no longer allow the Egyptian-Israeli relationship to consume all of his time, yet he felt bound to keep both Begin and Sadat aware of his personal interest and commitment. So he delegated his role in the negotiations not to the State Department or any other bureaucrat but to a "Personal Representative."

Carter's choice was Robert Strauss, a well-connected Texas Democrat who had just achieved a major triumph as his Special Trade Negotiator. Strauss thus had the reputation of a man with presidential clout. A Foreign Service professional, Ambassador James Leonard, was assigned as his Deputy to make sure that lines did not cross with Secretary of State Vance. But Strauss also had important limitations, an understandable ignorance of the issues being the least of them. He was a man in a hurry entering a situation where both sides were newly seized by caution and restraint.

Strauss's mandate to "fast-track" the negotiations was soon reduced to utter frustration. On the Israeli side, Begin had acted to make sure that autonomy did not get out of his hands. To reinforce both his concept that autonomy was a kind of Israeli "internal" matter and to shore up his parliamentary coalition, Begin arranged for a committee of cabinet officials, chaired by the chairman of the National Religious Party, the veteran politician Josef Burg, to conduct the negotiations. Burg, whose own party was badly split over retention of the territories, relied on Begin's direct guidance. Otherwise, he could not move at all. And, at the working group level, as one Israeli negotiator put it, "We did not have the flexibility even to nod our heads."

This extraordinary system claimed as its primary victim a moving spirit of Camp David, Foreign Minister Moshe Dayan. Dayan had reportedly been offered the chairmanship of the Israeli Committee but he declined. He could not lead the autonomy negotiations because he concluded that Begin, under pressure, did not intend autonomy to mean what he, Dayan, wanted it to mean. Begin's six-minister committee, among whom was the obviously disgruntled Moshe Dayan, thus became a "go-slow" device *par excellence.*

On the Egyptian side, Sadat's senior civil servants had been horrified at what he had wrought in the Camp David Accords. They wanted to protect him (and Egypt) from what they regarded as dangerous exposure to the wrath of the other Arab states. Meanwhile, Sadat himself expected the Americans, as "full partners," to do the heavy lifting on autonomy and much else, including the recruitment of other Arab support.

Strauss therefore found it difficult to get the parties even to agree on a agenda. After the opening session in May, he became increasingly disaffected from the entire exercise. At one point, his exasperation reportedly found a colorful expression: "It's like trying to wipe your rear with a wheel," he complained. "It goes round and round and nothing happens." Finally, the "agenda" problem was resolved by dividing into two committees (or commissions), one on procedures for elections which met with rapid progress, the other on the powers to be granted the self-governing authority, where there was no progress at all.

Strauss's discomfiture was complete when the Carter Administration resumed its search for the Holy Grail of PLO support, given untimely impetus by events in the Persian Gulf. After overthrowing the Shah in early 1979, the Ayatollah Khomeini had turned Iran into an aggressively anti-American force that, unlike its imperial predecessor, denounced the Camp David Accords and enjoyed close ties to the PLO. To shore up Arab opposition to Iran and to diffuse the Ayatollah's appeal, Camp David's base of support needed broadening and that included dividing the Arab Rejectionist Front, led by Iraq.[1] It was also thought that a signal of Palestinian support would loosen Egypt's reluctance to negotiate on their behalf. All of this led the Carter Administration to favor a new Security Council Resolution, which would reaffirm UN Security Council Resolution 242, but add some phraseology to satisfy the PLO's complaint that 242 was unacceptable because it mentioned the Palestinians only as refugees.

---

[1]For the details of this episode see Harvey Sicherman, "American Policy in the Middle East 1978-79," *Middle East Contemporary Survey,* Volume III: 1978-79, (New York: Holmes and Meier, 1979), pp. 23-25.

Strauss, sent to explain how all of this would help Camp David, met outrage in Jerusalem. In Cairo, Sadat affably concluded that doing this was "stupid." Both Egypt and Israel were now alarmed that the United States was somehow backing off of the Accords to placate their enemies. To reassure them, Washington abruptly reversed course, but not before the U.S. Ambassador to the UN, civil rights leader Andrew Young, violated the pledge against negotiating directly with the PLO. Young's subsequent resignation—attributed to Jewish pressure—greatly embittered Jewish-Black relations, harming Carter's own Democratic Party. Suddenly, the President's Middle East policies were becoming a huge domestic liability just as his reelection effort was getting under way.

Completely frustrated after six rounds of ministerial level meetings, Strauss resigned to run Carter's reelection campaign. In December 1979, Sol Linowitz, a Washington lawyer and successful businessman active in both Democratic politics and the Jewish community, was appointed as Carter's second "Personal Representative of the President for the Middle East Negotiations." Like Strauss, Linowitz had also recently conducted a successful negotiation, the Panama Canal Treaties. The President, however, left him with no illusions about what he faced in his new assignment.

Linowitz quickly detected that autonomy really depended for its constructive impulse on the top leaders. As the President's personal representative, he adopted what he called a "free wheeling" style of dealing with those leaders "one-on-one," spending little time in formal negotiating sessions with the cabinet level or working groups. He found Sadat "charged up" but curiously detached from his own government, whose senior officials were often unaware of what he was doing. The Egyptian leader urged haste and believed that a decent deal for the Palestinians would bring them along. "Tell my cousin Menachem not to stop in the middle of the road" was his message to Linowitz for Begin.[2]

Begin for his part was cautious, increasingly fettered to his coalition and determined, through Burg and his committee, to keep absolute control through every stage of negotiation. As we have seen, the first victim of this approach was Foreign Minister Moshe Dayan who resigned in October 1979, in large

---

[2]Linowitz interview.

part because of differences over autonomy. Dayan later wrote that Begin wanted autonomy in the framework of Israeli sovereignty while he, Dayan, believed "that we had to establish a pattern of relationship between us and the Palestinians that would preserve our vital interests, and at the same time enable the Arabs to lead their lives as they wished." In Dayan's opinion, this excluded a Palestinian state, required an Israeli military presence and allowed Israeli settlements "confined to uncultivated state land or land bought by us from its Arab owners."[3]

Linowitz did not regard Begin's approach as incompatible with agreement on an interim arrangement. Begin insisted that "functional self-government" for the Palestinians not touch the spheres of security or sovereignty, but Linowitz felt that this still gave considerable room for maneuver. And he also found Dayan's successor, Yitzhak Shamir, who became Foreign Minister in March 1980, to be helpful in dealing with Begin.

In early January of 1980, a Begin-Sadat meeting failed to make any headway on autonomy. Sadat, still intent on speed, wanted to try the scheme first in Gaza, an idea that he pursued despite Israeli opposition and the murder six months earlier of a prominent Egyptian supporter there by a Syrian supported Palestinian terrorist group, the Popular Front for the Liberation of Palestine. Rather than pursue this barren line, Linowitz got the Israelis and the Egyptians to present "models" of what they meant by self-government or autonomy.[4] The models were to draw upon the actual workings of the Israeli Military Government.

The **Israeli model** proposed an eleven member Administrative Council (including the Chairman). Its local divisions were clearly "functional," i.e. education, health, religious, commerce, etc. Perhaps the most important feature of this model was the division of powers into three categories: **exclusive** to the Self-Governing Authority (Administrative Council); **shared** by the SGA (AC) and Israel; **"residual"** powers remaining with Israel. The Israeli approach assigned

---

[3]See Moshe Dayan, *Breakthrough*, (New York: Alfred Knopf, 1981), pp. 303-304.

[4]See Appendices VI and VII for the full Israeli and Egyptian models.

the SGA (AC) exclusive powers according to functional division.

The **Egyptian model**, like the Israeli, drew upon the actual workings of the Israeli Military Government's so-called Civil Administration. While admitting the distinction between legislative and executive power, the Egyptians proposed that **both** be turned over to the SGA (AC), the "withdrawal of the Israeli Military Government and its Civilian Administration" being required by Camp David. With telling bureaucratic precision, the Egyptians pointed out that the Civil Administration was already a mostly Palestinian run-affair (in 1978, there were 11,165 Palestinian employees compared to 980 Israelis in the West Bank; each of the Directors-General of the Gaza administration units was a Palestinian). It was therefore necessary under the new autonomy to give the Palestinians power to order themselves, not just to take orders from Israel as they did already.

Egypt's model made clear that Cairo was proposing a kind of Mandate for the development of an independent Palestine. Thus, a purpose of the SGA was to prepare Palestinians for final status and the right to self-determination; the SGA powers derived from itself, i.e. an independent body; its sway extended over both land and inhabitants, including Arab Jerusalem **and** Israeli settlements, which in the end must be withdrawn. There were to be 80 to 100 freely elected members to the Autonomy Authority's "Parliamentary Assembly." Egypt proposed that both the Assembly and its Executive Council (10-15 members elected from the Assembly) should be headquartered in East Jerusalem and able to issue "travel documents" and control travel—in short, the powers of a near-state. Only foreign policy and the military were excluded.

SPRING CRISIS

On January 30, the occasion of the eighth ministerial round, Linowitz selected the Israeli framework of powers—some powers exclusive to the Self-Governing Authority (Administrative Council); others shared by the SGA (AC) and Israel; and residual powers "remaining" with Israel—as the most creative way to pursue the talks. In his view, the functional assignment of powers would delineate the issues, show agreements and reveal the most important gaps. The

Egyptians resisted this approach because they did not care to go far into details which necessitated their making "concessions" at the expense of the Arabs not present. But by the ninth round on February 27-28, Cairo did agree. Simultaneously, the Israelis also allowed that there could be an informal discussion of security issues, which heretofore had been off the table. New committees on economics and legal matters were added to the existing bodies on elections and powers.

This progress, however, was soon overshadowed by events in the territories and elsewhere. The Carter Administration found itself beset by both the Iranian hostage crisis and then, in December 1979, by the Soviet invasion of Afghanistan. Iraq's Saddam Hussein (leader of the Arab Rejectionist Front) and the Ayatollah's Iran had begun the quarrel that would lead to full-scale war in September 1980. Camp David had attracted no new takers and in Washington the Middle East overall seemed out of control.

Even as the diplomats discussed autonomy, the situation in the West Bank and Gaza had deteriorated. Already in November of 1979, Israeli Defense Minister Ezer Weizman had attempted to expel Nablus Mayor Bassam Shakaa, an outspoken PLO supporter, who had been elected three years earlier in what all had agreed was a fair and honest poll. Weizman's decision was reversed under severe legal and political pressure but the Israelis continued to accumulate evidence against Shakaa and to prevent the mayors from meeting as a body to discuss broader political issues.

Then, on January 31, 1980, a Yeshiva student was murdered in Hebron's old city center. The Begin government seized this opportunity to allow more Jews to settle Hebron's Jewish quarter, which had been almost completely destroyed and many of its inhabitants massacred in the Arab revolt of 1929. This was followed on March 23 by the government's decision to establish a Yeshiva there. Two days later, a fierce public protest in Hebron marked the opening of a general strike throughout the territories.

On March 1, the United States voted for a unanimous UN Security Council Resolution that deplored Israel's settlement activity in the territories ". . . including Jerusalem" and called upon Israel to dismantle existing settlements. The Israelis were infuriated and Carter disavowed the vote; then the Arabs were furious. Meanwhile, American attempts to interest Jordan and the Palestinians in joining the autonomy talks had come up empty.

Amidst these violent circumstances, Sadat decided he must bring matters to a head. Both he and Begin had agreed to negotiate in good faith so that an autonomy agreement would be achieved within a year, the target date being May 26, 1980. But no agreement was in sight. It was, therefore, in Sadat's view, time for another Camp David to break the deadlock. His letter to Begin proposing such a summit also included these demands: voting rights for East Jerusalem Arabs; legislative authority for the autonomy; Israeli military movements only by consent of the autonomy self-government authority; and a freeze on Jewish settlements. Begin turned it all down and Carter invited each leader instead for a separate visit.

These visits yielded very little. Sadat obtained from Carter a pledge for a real Camp David if he were reelected. The U.S. could agree with some of Sadat's points—elections in East Jerusalem and a settlement freeze—but not with the notion that all powers should be transferred to the SGA. Begin insisted on functional administrative powers, of which he determined there were 13, and the election of 13 functionaries to exercise them; he rejected any foreign jurisdiction over Israeli settlers and restated Israel's role as "sole judge" of her security. He was agreeable, however, to a presentation of the Israeli defense concept in the autonomy negotiations. Finally, all sides resolved to continue intensive discussions in the hopes of completing something to mark the one-year deadline they had agreed upon.

Instead, May provided a month of disasters. On May 2, five Yeshiva students were killed and 17 wounded in an attack in Hebron. The Israeli authorities then expelled the most ardent pro-PLO leaders in the West Bank and Gaza. Three West Bank mayors were also badly maimed by settler vigilantes.

While security on the ground was thus visibly deteriorating, the autonomy negotiations took up "security concepts" in the eleventh ministerial round, held in Herzlia, Israel, from May 1-7. The talks were hedged with difficulties. Israel refused to set up the special security committee demanded by the Egyptians as a "precondition" for further negotiations; the talks were considered "informal" as a compromise, with security clearly on the agenda. Israel's presentation was delivered crisply by General Avraham

Tamir, who stressed Israel's intent to keep all security issues exclusively in its hands, including the location of its bases, until the final status of the West Bank and Gaza was determined.[5] On May 5 the Egyptians presented their concept: the autonomy authority must have exclusive security powers (police, anti-terror and even borders) in its control; there would be a formal territorial borderline between the autonomous areas and Israel; Israeli military forces could locate themselves and move around only with the permission of the SGA, pending full withdrawal after the interim period; and Israeli settlements would be dismantled. Finally, early warning stations would not necessarily be under total Israeli control. This was an astonishing and unwelcome surprise, and quite at variance with the Camp David Accords. Nonetheless a showdown was avoided when the Egyptian negotiators recharacterized their demands as suggestions. Talks were set to resume on May 12.

Sadat, however, postponed any further discussions because the Jerusalem issue had surfaced once more. Both the Egyptian and the Israeli parliaments had been busy stoking the fires of discord. Carter's reversal at the UN in March led the Egyptian People's Assembly to "fix" the matter by rejecting all Israeli changes in Arab Jerusalem, which in their view was also part of the West Bank. The Knesset for its part had extended Israeli law and jurisdiction to the city (sovereignty being assumed) some twelve years earlier in 1967. But for MK Geula Cohen of the Likud, this was not enough, and she offered a private member's bill reaffirming that decision, intended to rebut the UN, the U.S. and Egypt. When, on May 15, the Jerusalem Bill was referred by the Knesset to Committee, i.e., taken as a serious bill, Egypt suspended the autonomy negotiations. Begin subsequently announced that he would transfer his office to East Jerusalem.

---

[5]Some account of the Israeli approach is given in Ze'ev Schiff, *Security for Peace: Israel's Minimum Security Requirements in Negotiations with the Palestinians*, (Washington: The Washington Institute for Near East Policy, 1989), pp. 74-75. A detailed review of the autonomy negotiations at this stage, drawing on Israeli sources, is given by Moshe Gammar and Shimon Shamir in *Middle East Contemporary Survey*, Volume VI: 1980-1981, (New York: Holmes and Meier, 1981), pp. 117-124.

Linowitz was able to persuade Sadat that an unpassed bill should not be allowed to torpedo the entire autonomy project. But things did not get better. On June 13 the European Community passed a kind of peace plan that invited PLO participation. Carter tried desperately in early July to "bridge" some of the disputes, hoping to reinvigorate the Camp David process; he failed. Then on July 30, the Knesset passed the Jerusalem bill. Sadat promptly suspended the formal negotiations, leaving Linowitz with only a "shuttle" at his disposal.

The disastrous push of April and May had only emphasized the growing limitations constraining each of the Camp David parties. Carter faced a difficult renomination and election fight at home; the domestic economy was sour; and the administration was collecting a series of foreign policy reverses, in Iran, Afghanistan and Nicaragua. Sadat, ostracized by his fellow Arabs, disappointed by the lack of U.S. influence over Jordan and Saudi Arabia, also faced his own economic morass that U.S. aid had yet to alleviate. Begin was physically ailing and his fractious cabinet was barely under control.[6]

The Egyptian and American attempt to concert pressure on Begin had gone too far. The upshot was to confirm Begin's inclination to reduce the Self-Governing Authority to a "clerk's" council. Meanwhile, the situation in the territories aggravated these political mishaps and in turn was aggravated by them. As it had in the past—and would in the future—the Jerusalem issue was then exploited by the opponents of the entire process to make matters still worse.

Sometime in August, Sadat rediscovered the original logic of Camp David. The Egyptians (and also the Americans) had often argued that the Egyptian-Israeli peace would be affected by the outcome of the autonomy negotiations. But if there were no negotiations, there would certainly be no agreement. And in the absence of agreement would either Egypt or Israel refuse to honor the Peace Treaty? No one wanted to run the risk of finding out, at least not two years before the last stage of Israeli withdrawal from Sinai. And so, Sadat agreed with Linowitz that there was no point in not negotiating.

---

[6]In May, Ezer Weizman, Defense Minister and architect of Likud's stunning election victory in 1977, resigned, bitterly accusing Begin of failing in his responsibility to achieve a broader peace.

On October 18, 1980, Linowitz was able to convene another ministerial meeting. Egypt deemed it preparation for a summit while Israel took it as merely another installment of the talks. But both sides were determined to make the best of it.

Linowitz had resumed his original emphasis on obtaining agreement over the divisions of powers. On this occasion, his Israeli visitors brought him something new which appeared to indicate an Israeli desire for serious progress. Israel was now prepared to make **future** development of land and water subject to a shared power with the self-governing authority.[7] This presumably covered land not already set aside for military purposes and it implied a mutual veto that could certainly affect Israeli settlement plans. Linowitz did not explore the subject very far. He was happy to seize upon the principle of a shared power, leaving its precise meaning to be negotiated by Israel and its Arab partner—or partners if the Palestinians ever showed. The Egyptians, hewing rigidly to their previous lines, were unmoved.

A SUMMING UP

The Carter presidency ended with his overwhelming defeat by Ronald Reagan in November of 1980. In the Middle East, the Camp David partners offered glowing testimonials to the President and erstwhile peacemaker. Carter's monument— peace between Egypt and Israel—was established although not deeply rooted.

Special Negotiator Linowitz had emerged from his experience convinced that an autonomy negotiation was "do-able," and that the absence of Jordan and the Palestinians could be finessed by a deal that left details for them to negotiate. He regarded them as "affronted but pragmatic," awaiting an Israeli-Egyptian deal before deciding what to do next.[8] Indeed, a survey of West Bank and Gaza civic leaders taken by one

---

[7]Linowitz interview. See also Ruth Lapidoth, "The Camp David Process and the New U.S. Plan for the Middle East: A Legal Analysis," *USC Cites*, Fall-Winter 1982-83, p. 24. Lapidoth, then Legal Advisor to the Israeli negotiating team, wrote that "Israel apparently proposed" this shared power.

[8]Linowitz interview.

American analyst revealed acceptance of the interim period concept, so long as it was a step toward independence from Israel. Their ideas for Palestinian self-government included many of the powers the Israeli proposal would have granted plus of course many others that would have made the autonomy into a proto-state.[9]

Writing to Carter on January 14, 1981, Linowitz offered a public summation of what had been achieved. [See Appendix VIII for the report] He found agreement on election procedures, but not on the participation of "Palestinian inhabitants of Jerusalem"; narrowed differences on the size and structure of the Self-Governing Authority (Administrative Council); and "at least" twenty-five (25) areas and functions for SGA (AC) responsibility. These corresponded to Israel's list of powers exclusive to the Self-Governing Authority, some of which were combined by the Israelis to make their list of 13 (e.g. "Industry, Commerce, Tourism" are listed as one in the Israeli Proposal and listed separately as three in the Linowitz report).

Linowitz also laid out the five major areas of disagreement:
(1) Nature and source of powers—legislative or administrative?
(2) Water and Land rights—how would they be shared?
(3) Jewish settlements
(4) Security
(5) East Jerusalem

The report hinted at the Israeli water and land proposals, noting that on water both Egypt and Israel agreed "that both the inhabitants [of the territories] and Israel share an essential stake in the disposition of those water resources which underlie both the territories and Israel and to that end coordination between them will be necessary." The report also announced that the parties planned a Continuing Committee (the U.S. was invited to join and Jordan urged to participate) to decide "on the modalities of admission of persons displaced in 1967 . . . " Quoting the joint Begin-Sadat declaration of December 13, 1980, that Camp David remained "the only viable path toward comprehensive peace in the Middle East today," Linowitz concluded "that it is in the highest interest of

---

[9]*Journal of Palestine Studies,* Volume IX, No. 3, Spring 1980, pp. 189-91. The survey was conducted by Dr. Ann Lesch and published originally in *The Link* (November-December 1979).

the United States to press forward in the weeks and months ahead in order to conclude the negotiations at the earliest possible date."

IV BAD LUCK AND BAD TIMING: 1981-82

Linowitz's conclusion did not stimulate immediate action by the newly-elected Reagan Administration. Its foreign policy priorities were "to stand tall" and especially to halt the expansion of Soviet influence. Aside from this emphasis, President Reagan himself was mainly concerned during his early months in office with reviving the American spirit, stimulating the economy, and enlarging the defense budget, not the conduct of international relations.

As for the Middle East, Reagan had a strong and heartfelt interest in Israel, a country he characterized as a strategic ally. While some of his circle—notably Caspar Weinberger, the Secretary of Defense—did not share this enthusiasm, none of the new President's advisors possessed the Carter team's zeal for redressing Palestinian grievances. Reagan thus had no particular political stake or personal interest in autonomy.

His first Secretary of State, Alexander M. Haig Jr., had considerable experience in the region. He had met most of the players—including Begin—during the Nixon Administration when he had been Deputy to Kissinger at the National Security Council and later Nixon's chief of staff. Also strongly supportive of Israel, Haig, like the President, was primarily concerned with reversing Soviet influence.

Haig was under no illusions that the Soviet threat would submerge the Arab-Israeli conflict. He believed instead that by solidifying the Egyptian-Israeli peace, and somehow adding Saudi Arabia's tacit support to it, the Soviets and their local friends, including Syria, could be thwarted. This approach had received an important boost when Iraq invaded Iran in

September 1980, neutralizing at a stroke both of the most powerful local antagonists to Camp David. The Saudis for their part were now much in need of American assistance and less subject to Iraqi intimidation once Saddam Hussein was embroiled with the Ayatollah.

Haig described what he thought he had found in the Middle East as a "consensus of strategic concern." By that he meant that America's friends in the area, even if they would not work well with each other, might be willing to work with the U.S. to deal with the danger of Soviet influence. It was then up to the U.S. to "coordinate" these plans. "Strategic consensus" justified the controversial U.S. sale of Advanced Warning And Communications System aircraft (AWACS) to Saudi Arabia in 1981 and an equally controversial attempt to make Israel a formal "strategic ally." Eventually the groundwork was laid for regular military exercises, prepositioning and overbuilding of certain facilities, and intelligence sharing, all of which proved to be essential a decade later when Saddam Hussein, rather than the USSR, challenged U.S. interests.

The Palestinian problem figured only on a secondary level for both Haig and Reagan. The President saw the PLO as a terrorist operation while Haig saw no point in soliciting Arafat, especially not as a substitute for a more robust policy in the Gulf. Nor was the new Administration much exercised over Palestinian grievances and claims. Early on, the President called the settlements "not illegal." Professor Eugene V. Rostow, an eminent legal scholar then serving as Director of the Arms Control and Disarmament Agency, had argued that because the West Bank and Gaza were "an unallocated part of the British Mandate," the settlements were legal and the argument over them political.[1] Whatever the legalities (or the illegalities) Reagan and Haig came to oppose the settlements as impediments to the peace process, but they decided to take it up quietly with the Israelis.[2] This was a highly unwelcome

[1]See Eugene V. Rostow, "Bricks and Stones," *The New Republic*, April 23, 1990. For a lengthier exposition, see "Palestinian Self-Determination: Possible Futures for the Unallocated Territories of the Palestine Mandate," Yale Studies in World Public Order, Volume V, 1979, p. 147 *et passim.*

[2]In October 1991, a former State Department official, David Korn, alleged that the illegality charge had deterred Israel's settlement drive (modestly) and that by dropping the point, the Reagan Administration

change for the Arabs who had come to expect a periodic U.S.-Israeli brawl on the subject, especially at the U.N.[3]

RESTARTING AUTONOMY

Autonomy's place in all of this was, then, not as a device to attract the PLO but rather a means of solidifying the Egyptian-Israeli relationship, a key U.S. strength in the Middle East. Haig did not believe that Camp David could ever satisfy Arafat's demand for independence and saw no point in trying to portray it as a corridor to a Palestinian state. His State Department Middle East experts, many of whom preferred a Palestinian state or a Jordanian-Palestinian federative solution, fell in with this readily enough. They strove to keep the "options" open for an alternative once autonomy failed: a breakthrough in U.S.-PLO relations.[4]

Linowitz's enthusiasm—he told Haig the negotiations could be finished by May—was also not widely shared, if only because his final report to Carter showed that very large differences remained on most of the really critical issues. Moreover, the Special Negotiator 's role could not be the same as before. It symbolized Carter's unique presidential interest

---

also ceased to oppose Israeli settlement building in a crucial period. (See *The New York Times,* October 6, 1991). There is no evidence that American charges of "illegality" ever prevented any Israeli settlement. Korn was also unaware of the higher level U.S.-Israeli exchanges on the settlements.

[3]See Allan Gerson, *The Kirkpatrick Mission: Diplomacy Without Apology, America at the United Nations, 1981-1985,* (New York: The Free Press, 1991), pp. 57-68.

[4]This was the background to the so-called Mroz affair. In August 1981, Professor John Mroz, of the International Peace Academy in New York, initiated an unofficial contact between State Department officials and PLO leader Yasser Arafat. Haig authorized the discussion with Mroz so long as the 1975 U.S. promises to Israel were kept, but he has neither record nor recollection of any "messages" that emerged from this channel. Mroz's activities (which continued until May 1982) were apparently nurtured by higher-level State Department officials long after the original authorization. Personal Interview with Secretary of State Haig. Also, see *The New York Times,* February 18, 1984, and *Facts On File,* Volume 44, #2258, February 24, 1984.

and, in some respects, his penchant for details, qualities that Reagan did not share. Haig and the White House also fell quickly into a public quarrel over how foreign policy was to be made and who was to conduct it, especially in times of crisis. Then Reagan was nearly assassinated in late March, and his wounds severely curtailed his work schedule for months.

These circumstances convinced Haig that continuing to negotiate through a Special Negotiator directly responsible to the President would be both impractical and unwise. And, in any event, as Haig discovered on his first visit to Cairo in April, 1981, there was another, far more important and insuperable barrier to a "fast start" on autonomy: Sadat refused to resume any discussions on the subject until after the Israeli election then scheduled for June 1981. Like many in Washington, Sadat was hoping that Begin would be defeated by his Labour rival, Shimon Peres.

The American visitors found Sadat strangely detached from Egypt's extremely serious economic problems (there had been rioting in January 1981 when Cairo attempted to carry out an IMF reform program) and totally disdainful of his critics both abroad and at home. Sadat told Haig he had gone to Jerusalem because he feared American *naivete* about the Soviets would jeopardize everything he had sought in the peace process. He readily agreed with Haig's anti-Soviet strategy of strategic consensus and saw a major role for Egypt in it. If anything, Sadat outdid the Americans in denouncing the Soviets: he saw Moscow making a three pronged attempt through its Iraqi ally, through proxies in Yemen, Ethiopia and Libya, and through support for Syria, to isolate and overthrow him. But Sadat also expressed his disappointment with America's failure to "produce" more Arab support for Camp David or to finish the autonomy negotiations.[5]

In Israel that April, Haig found the opposite approach to autonomy. Ariel Sharon had suddenly surfaced as a proponent of rapid progress, arguing that the talks could be settled in a few months if only the U.S. would "force" Egypt to resume negotiations in good faith. Beneath the surface could be detected Israel's desire to settle all outstanding issues with Egypt before her remaining forces were withdrawn on schedule from Sinai in April of 1982.

---

[5]Haig interview.

With American encouragement, Begin and Sadat met on June 4, 1981 at Gezira in Southern Sinai. But three days later on June 7, Israel bombed Iraq's nascent nuclear program at Osirak, greatly embarrassing the Egyptians and earning widespread condemnation abroad, which included a hostile UN resolution and a slowdown in the supply of U.S. war planes to Israel by Secretary of Defense Weinberger. Despite pre-election public opinion polls showing a Peres lead, Begin's Likud emerged as the largest Israeli party once more when the votes were tallied on June 30, 1981.

Begin's second government contained a different and far more difficult array of personalities for the United States. Dayan and Weizman were gone. The new Foreign Minister Yitzhak Shamir had opposed the Camp David Accords. The new Defense Minister Ariel Sharon had disturbed the earlier peace negotiations with theatrical bulldozing of new settlement sites in Sinai. As the official now in charge of the West Bank and Gaza, Sharon argued that Palestinian aspirations to statehood could be satisfied in Jordan, which he claimed was already a Palestinian state. He was prepared to take forceful action against the local leadership, much as he had done in putting down a rebellion in Gaza ten years earlier. And he proposed a much broader settlement plan, which would place Jewish settlements not only on the possible invasion routes from the south and east but between major Arab population centers, foreclosing the possibility of a contiguous Palestinian polity even in the West Bank.

In early August of 1981, Sadat visited Washington to bask in the new administration's support. During Sadat's visit, Saudi Arabia's Crown Prince Fahd unexpectedly launched an alternative to Camp David.[6] Couched as an "international consensus," the Prince's remarks suggested a return to the Arab version of 242. Fahd's plan also contained a transition period for the West Bank, this time under UN supervision. The "Fahd Plan" was an unusual Saudi bid for a new Arab rapprochement; Sadat did not dismiss it, although he wondered aloud how the Saudis could advance it in the absence of any negotiations with Israel. Some in the Reagan Administration expressed considerable interest in the plan.

---

[6]Text can be found in *Middle East Contemporary Survey*, Volume V: 1980-81, (New York: Holmes and Meier, 1981), pp. 163-65.

Soon thereafter on August 25-26, 1981, Sadat and Begin met in Alexandria to reaffirm their partnership on the basis of Camp David. By all accounts, it was the best meeting they ever experienced. Both sides liked the American consensus idea. Both also resolved to reinforce their relationship by speeding up "normalization" and finishing the autonomy negotiations no later than year's end, well ahead of the final Sinai withdrawal scheduled for April 26, 1982. Informed of this surprising and welcome development, Haig instructed that his calendar be cleared for a three to six week "shuttle" in November-December, 1981.

The Alexandria Summit cleared the way for the resumption, on September 23-24, of the official autonomy negotiations in Giza, a Cairo suburb. Nearly a year had passed since the issues had been encountered. There being no Special Negotiator , the American Ambassadors to Egypt and Israel, Alfred Atherton and Samuel Lewis, co-chaired the U.S. delegation at what turned out to be a productive meeting. Further sessions were scheduled for October and both sides agreed to pursue "principles" of autonomy rather than the precise detail Israel had previously demanded and the Egyptians detested. This promised much faster movement.

SADAT'S MURDER: CAMP DAVID UNDER SIEGE

The entire edifice of the peace process was badly shaken, however, when on October 6, 1981 Sadat was murdered by Egyptian soldiers belonging to a radical Muslim group while reviewing a parade commemorating the Yom Kippur War. The Camp David Accords were now put to the test. Would Egypt and Israel hold to their commitment? And would Washington hold to Camp David?

Haig had been working to put in place the final prerequisite of an Israeli withdrawal—a multinational force for Sinai as required by the Treaty. He was now confronted by European and Saudi attempts to supercede Camp David in favor of either the European Community's international conference (including the PLO) or the Fahd Plan. A savage argument erupted behind the scenes, especially with the British, over whether the Europeans would join the multinational force without attaching political conditions that would invoke the EC scheme. Haig argued strongly that in the absence of unconditional European participation, the entire Egyptian-Israeli Peace Treaty could be in jeopardy. Israel would simply not leave Sinai if Camp David was to be denied. After he arranged direct appeals from Reagan to British Prime Minister Margaret Thatcher and French President Francois Mitterand, both agreed on November 22, 1981 to join the Force under the Camp David Framework—overruling their foreign ministries. The Peace Treaty had been saved.

The new Egyptian President, Hosni Mubarak, had been Sadat's vice president, and he insisted that Sadat's policy would continue. But he made several swift adjustments. He released most of the opposition politicians Sadat had arrested shortly before his assassination and severely repressed Islamic fundamentalist cells throughout Egypt. Mubarak also agreed to continue the autonomy negotiations but, as soon became evident, without giving his negotiators a mandate to compromise.

The autonomy working team met in Tel Aviv from October 23-29 and then, on November 4-12, a ministerial round was held at Giza. In between Egyptian Foreign Minister Kamal Hassan Ali visited Begin and reaffirmed the importance of the Camp David Accords although they made no particular progress on autonomy except to emphasize the election modalities. In the course of the ministerial sessions the Israelis suggested that the future development of land and water be a shared power. While this was not new, Linowitz having heard it the year before, it was regarded as highly significant by the U.S. team, given the Begin government's composition and Sharon's role as Defense Minister in charge of the territories.[7]

---

[7]Official Israeli autonomy proposals as published [See Appendix IX] do **not** contain this position. Some hint of them is given in public comments at the time by Yitzhak Shamir and for the opposition, Yitzhak Rabin. See also Ruth Lapidoth, "The Camp David Process and the New U.S. Plan for the Middle East: A Legal Analysis," *USC Cites*, Fall-Winter 1982-83, p. 24. Various U.S. participants in the autonomy negotiations, including Former Secretary of State Haig, confirm that Israel did put future land and water development as a shared power "on the table" in late 1981-early 1982. One diplomat attached to the U.S. embassy at the time, however, suggested that Begin in particular was most anxious to finish the negotiations and took positions "ahead of" his party—testing the waters before going public. See FBIS January 22, 1982 for Rabin's January 13th description of Sharon's water-land proposal as "flexible" and "acceptable" to Labour. In a lengthy interview on January 28, 1982

The Americans found, however, that the Egyptians were oddly unreceptive to this manifestation of Israel's willingness to share some important powers with the Palestinians. The ministerial meeting was rather taken up mostly with Israel's insistence that Egypt reaffirm once more its devotion to the Accords as the "sole framework" for progress, a point clearly intended to prevent any Egyptian dallying with the Fahd Plan or the Europeans. Convinced from the Egyptian stance in the talks that Mubarak wanted no further exposure on the Palestinian issue, the Israelis concluded by November 15 that an autonomy agreement could not be concluded any time soon.[8]

On December 14th, Begin's unexpected application of Israeli law and jurisdiction to the Golan Heights (regarded by other countries as virtual annexation) distracted all attention from the talks. Many members of the U.S. team had already concluded that Washington's interest lay elsewhere and that autonomy was an orphan. This was only partly true. Having sustained Camp David despite Sadat's murder and these other disasters, Haig—along with Begin and Mubarak—still had a profound reason to focus on autonomy: if the negotiations were allowed to wither, the impending final Israeli withdrawal from Sinai might be upset.

Haig's first foreign trip in January 1982 took him to Europe, where he rallied opposition to the Communist imposition of martial law against the Solidarity Union in Poland. Upon reaching Cairo on January 12, Haig found that his plan to press the autonomy talks to a rapid conclusion was subtly opposed by the Egyptians, who had resumed their most rigid positions that autonomy was the prelude to Palestinian sovereignty. In

---

(Foreign Broadcast Information Service [FBIS] January 29, 1982) Shamir described the Israeli proposal on land as having received "many compliments" from the U.S. because, in Shamir's view, it offered "great consideration" for the Arab inhabitants. The Hebrew newspaper *Ma'ariv* published a version of the full Israeli plan which, like all public Israeli plans, did not refer specifically to water or land as a shared power but assigned powers to the Self-Governing Authority while referring vaguely to activities that require "cooperation" and "coordination."

[8] See Moshe Gammer, "Egyptian-Israeli Relations," *Middle East Contemporary Survey*, Volume VI: 1981-82, p.162.

Jerusalem a day later, the focus was different. The Israelis were nervous about both Sinai and Lebanon. Begin and Sharon were full of warnings about Egyptian behavior and the risks of war with the PLO and Syria. The Secretary of State was nonetheless able to discuss the ramifications of the "shared land development" proposal, probing whether this would cover military areas that would come free once Israeli forces had been withdrawn to select sites as required by Camp David.[9] But both Burg and Begin gave him to understand that an autonomy agreement was not really within reach.[10]

THE THIRD SPECIAL NEGOTIATOR

Returning to Washington, Haig faced a serious dilemma. Where before, Egypt and the U.S. suggested that lack of agreement on autonomy might hamper the Peace Treaty while Israel resisted, more recently Israel had been arguing that autonomy should be settled lest it complicate withdrawal from Sinai.

Sadat's murder, the difficulties over the multinational force in Sinai and the danger of war in Lebanon stoked fears that all could yet be lost if the withdrawal was not carried out. A crisis over autonomy had to be avoided, yet agreement was nowhere in sight. Egypt would take no further risks. And Begin and Sharon had come to believe that even after the Sinai withdrawal, autonomy could not be workable so long as the PLO continued to thrive as both a diplomatic force and as a

---

[9]Haig interview. U.S. working-level morale at this juncture was not very high, something that Haig himself noticed. One member of the team recalled a stupefying discussion over whether the Self-Governing Authority (Administrative Council) could issue postage stamps—perhaps a sign of sovereignty. Haig himself had a taste of what could happen when he and Begin had a go-around on the size of the autonomy council. When Haig suggested that 20 or 30 was a good compromise (versus Egypt's proposed 80-100) and corresponding to Linowitz's 25 powers, Begin demurred. He had learned that a certain European state had a parliament of that size; thirteen was therefore a better number, corresponding to the functional activities of the SGA (AC) as defined in the latest Israeli proposal. Despite such incidents, both the Israeli and the U.S. teams did make important progress in narrowing differences over the difficult 1981-82 period.

[10]Haig interview.

growing military problem on Israel's northern border. Haig had therefore to extricate the U.S. and its partners from further frictions on autonomy without collapsing the negotiations altogether.

Returning to Cairo and Jerusalem on January 27-29, the Secretary of State worked on convincing Israel to accept European troops in the Sinai Multinational Force despite a final flurry of inflammatory statements from various European foreign ministries. He also began work on the absurd Taba dispute which was to curse Egyptian-Israeli relations for years thereafter.[11] Finally, Haig introduced Richard Fairbanks, a well-connected Republican lawyer then serving as State Department Counsellor, who was to become the third Special Negotiator. This was Haig's solution to the immediate autonomy dilemma. Fairbanks' task was to keep the talks alive but free of friction and to sort them out for a later Haig effort once Sinai withdrawal had taken place. His was a novel and quite different role than had been played by Strauss and Linowitz.

Fairbanks, like Linowitz, soon came to believe that autonomy made sense, was "doable" and could be done fairly quickly if the parties could be made to focus on it. He also thought that the Palestinians had a lot to gain from it all, a prospect of which they were ignorant because of lack of accurate information and false hopes of rescue by the PLO or the international community. Sharon inadvertently aided Fairbank's cause. As part of an attempt to undermine the PLO throughout the territories, Sharon took up "Village Leagues" as an alternative to the PLO-dominated city leadership, putting important patronage in the hands of rural Palestinians sometimes resentful of their urban brothers. This directly threatened the urban political class, including the PLO's base of

---

[11]Taba was a tiny strip of land astride the new Israel–Egyptian border and the site of an Israeli-owned resort hotel. The Israelis argued that the real demarcation line differed from official maps based on the 1914 British survey; the Egyptians cited the survey line and insisted that there could not be an adjustment to this border, the Israeli commercial interest notwithstanding. National pride thus engaged, years passed until the third party arbitration procedure was invoked, as provided under the Peace Treaty. Egypt was awarded the strip and a bitter aftertaste was left in all mouths.

support, to whom autonomy began to look like a way to frustrate Sharon's plans.

As was so often the case in this doleful history, procedure soon came to obstruct all else, provoked by the perennial quarrel over Jerusalem. Following the Sinai withdrawal, Mubarak was expected to visit Israel and thereby renew the "normalization" of the peace, so important a feature of the original Camp David bargain. But he refused to come if it meant a visit to Jerusalem. In the ensuing uproar, Begin declared that the next round of the autonomy negotiations should be held in Israel's capital. Egypt refused. Not a month after his first official visit to the area as a Special Negotiator (February 18-21), Fairbanks could only shuttle about while tempers cooled and some face-saving formula was devised.

On May 26, Haig delivered a speech on the Middle East that emphasized the need for diplomatic movement on three fronts: Lebanon, autonomy and the Iran-Iraq war. Although unable to interest the White House in any concrete initiatives, he was still persuaded that if the parties could only keep to the Camp David concept of autonomy as an interim agreement intended to improve Israeli-Palestinian relations, then at least that could be done. Fairbanks, through the diplomatic device of "non-papers" (unofficial statements of positions on the basis of informal discussions) had established the main areas of agreement and disagreement, areas closely resembling those of the late Linowitz period. He and Haig had planned tentatively for a Camp David-style meeting at the ministerial level for the eastern shore of Maryland sometime in June. Various "bridging proposals" had been developed at the working level that Fairbanks believed might offer ground for compromise, although they had not been discussed in detail with Haig.

The American working group was actually preparing to go from Israel to Egypt for another round of "non-papering" when the Lebanon War broke out. Haig was in Europe with President Reagan for the Versailles Summit of the leading industrial democracies. Summoned at 7:30 a.m. on June 6, to the State Department "situation room," Fairbanks ordered the group withdrawn.

Haig had only one more scene to play on autonomy before his embittered relations with the Reagan team on the Lebanon War compelled his resignation. On June 20-22, Prime Minister

Begin visited Washington. He was treated to criticism by the President but emerged more determined than ever to stay the course even though contrary to his original plan (and to the Israeli Cabinet's decisions) Ariel Sharon's Operation "Peace for Galilee" now involved the siege of Beirut and war with Syria.[12]

At a final meeting in Washington, Haig listened to Begin's explanation of how the destruction of the PLO in Lebanon would facilitate autonomy for the Palestinians in the territories. Haig then argued that if this was so, Israel could afford a more expansive version of powers for the autonomy once the PLO threat was removed. Promising to help hold the line for Israel in Washington, the Secretary of State suggested that after the war Begin should agree to U.S. bridging positions on some of the more contentious autonomy problems; he also argued strenuously for a settlements freeze to facilitate the negotiations, as Begin had done earlier following Camp David. Begin did not reject Haig's points but he did not accept them either.[13]

Haig had hoped that Israel, working with the U.S., could take the diplomatic offensive and secure a political victory commensurate with its military triumph, i.e., an autonomy agreement following the defeat of Syria and the PLO, and the freeing of Lebanon. But none of this was to be. On June 25, 1982, Haig resigned under pressure from the White House. Very soon thereafter the United States sharply opposed Israel's purposes in Lebanon. And on August 16, 1982, at the height of the siege of Beirut, Egypt announced its suspension of the autonomy negotiations pending Israeli withdrawal from Lebanon and a "new concept" for the discussions. True to form, the Egyptian-Israeli Peace Treaty survived Lebanon, but autonomy did not. [See Appendix IX for Israel's Final Autonomy Proposal]

---

[12]See Ze'ev Schiff and Ehud Yaari, *Israel's Lebanon War*, (New York: Simon and Schuster, 1984), p. 181 *et passim.*

[13]Haig interview.

THE REAGAN PLAN AND AUTONOMY

Haig had believed that the Israeli military action in
Lebanon, although going far beyond its originally announced
objective, could yield beneficial strategic results: A
humiliating defeat for the PLO and the Syrians would
seriously damage Soviet interests, Lebanon might be given a
chance to recover independence, and last but not least, the
Arab Rejectionist Front opposed to Camp David would be
crippled.

All of this depended, however, on a swift Israeli victory and
an equally swift removal of all foreign forces, Israeli, PLO and
Syrian, from Lebanon. But Sharon's strategy suffered from
flaws of both design and execution. His Christian allies failed
to take Beirut for him, leaving Israel to besiege the city and the
PLO. Nor were the Syrians driven out, although their severe air
losses and inadequate air defenses forced them into an early
cease-fire. Haig had then attempted to use the threat of further
Israeli military action to leverage agreements removing all
foreign forces and, with that accomplished, to deploy a
multinational force to stabilize Beirut, pending the
establishment of a new Lebanese government.

It did not work out that way. The new Secretary of State,
George Shultz, began by taking up the Palestinian issue; a U.S.
led multinational force was deployed to allow the PLO a
graceful exit; and the Syrians, anxious to be rearmed by the
Soviets, were not put under political pressure to agree to
anything until nearly mid-winter when new, more advanced
Soviet missiles were in place. By May of 1983, when the
stillborn Israel-Lebanon Peace Treaty was brokered personally
by Shultz, it was already clear that the Rejectionists—
especially Assad of Syria—were stronger than before.

This is not the place to recount the full Lebanon tragedy.
Suffice it to say that the Reagan Administration was anxious to
collect the strategic benefits of Syrian and PLO defeat while
simultaneously distancing the United States from an Israeli
government it considered dangerously out of control. Once the
PLO had been escorted out of Beirut the time was considered
ripe for a "U.S. plan" to resolve the unending drama of the
Palestinians. Its purpose would be to expand the circle of the
peacemakers with an overt appeal to the King of Jordan who
could now operate relatively free of Syrian and PLO

constraint—or so it was thought. Simultaneously, neither the State Department nor the White House wanted to abandon Camp David, which remained a restraint on Begin. Special efforts were therefore made to couch the American plan in terms of Camp David and especially in the context of the suspended autonomy negotiations.

Already on August 30, King Hussein, speaking in London, had hinted broadly at a forthcoming American initiative, adding what should have disturbed American officialdom but did not: any new U.S. proposals should present a clear break with Camp David. He had been thoroughly consulted by Assistant Secretary of State Nicholas Veliotes, a former U.S. ambassador to Jordan. Begin was not consulted on the initiative. In fact, Reagan's speech was hurriedly put together for fear that a leak would provoke a premature Israeli reaction. U.S. Ambassador to Israel Samuel Lewis described the results in these terms:

> The Reagan initiative on September 1 was a genuine effort to recreate momentum, to relaunch the Camp David agreement, with some embellishments, but fundamentally on the same terms. The timing was, in my judgment, abysmal, the tactics of its presentation worse, the outcome so far, nil.[14]

Lewis, in fact, had been compelled to present the ideas of the Reagan plan in a letter to a surprised Prime Minister Begin the day Reagan delivered his speech. Even worse, Lewis had been instructed to read the accompanying explanations or "talking points," without change [See Appendix X]. These were clearly written for Arab rather than Israeli ears, Washington's idea being to treat everyone to the identical message as an act of good faith.

Begin's vacation—for him a unique occasion—was interrupted to receive the Ambassador's urgent message. While quite aware of anger against him in Washington, the Israeli leader had believed that the ending of the Lebanon War

---

[14]Unofficial transcript of Ambassador Lewis' speech at the Dayan Center, Tel Aviv University, October 30, 1984, provided to the author by the Ambassador, who noted that Israeli press reports of his remarks— typically billed as "off the record"—got him into some ill-repute with the Reagan White House.

still left U.S. interests well ahead of where they had been before the Israeli invasion. He was in for a rude surprise.

The proposals themselves [See Appendix XI] reaffirmed Camp David and took the form of a commentary on "the positions we [the U.S.] will adopt in negotiations." As far as "transitional measures" this meant: 1) full autonomy meant "real authority" for the Palestinian inhabitants "over themselves, the land and its resources, subject to fair safeguards on water"; 2) new emphasis on the ties between the territories and Jordan; 3) East Jerusalem participation in the elections; 4) a real settlements freeze; and 5) most suggestive of all, "progressive Palestinian responsibility for internal security based on capability and performance." Some of the sting of these provisions for Israel was blunted by declarations that the U.S. would "oppose" threats to Israel's security ("reasonably defined"); isolation of the territories from Israel; and "sovereign rights" for either side during transition. External security had to remain in Israeli hands. The U.S. also stood against dismantling the existing settlements.

Having thus put the United States behind several of what had been the Fairbanks' bridging proposals, the U.S. paper then laid out positions on issues of final status. These were restatements of Washington's traditional position on 242, ("land for peace") although relieved by the President's public comment that Israel would never have to return to the vulnerable borders of 1967. It put the U.S. on record against either Israeli sovereignty or a Palestinian state for the West Bank and Gaza: "The preference we will pursue in the final status negotiations is association of the West Bank and Gaza with Jordan." While opposing once more the code words "self-determination" because they meant a Palestinian state, the U.S. took the Camp David language a step forward: "We believe that the Palestinians must take the leading role in determining their own future" versus the Camp David language of "the Palestinians will participate in the determination of their own future." Jerusalem would remain subject to negotiations. The talking points stated that Washington would not support Israeli settlement as "extraterritorial outposts."[15]

---

[15]Eight days after Reagan's speech and talking points, Secretary Shultz told the House Foreign Affairs committee that the U.S. position on settlements did not mean a denial of Jewish rights to live in the

Finally, Begin was informed that the King of Jordan understood the U.S. position that Camp David must remain the basis for negotiations, and that the U.S. would support these positions even if there were no takers. If there were, however, "the U.S. would take immediate steps to relaunch the autonomy negotiations with the broadest possible participation as envisaged under the Camp David Agreements."

Israel was seriously divided over the Reagan proposals. On September 4, the Begin government accused the U.S. of sharp "deviations" from Camp David and refused to negotiate the new proposals, while Shimon Peres announced for Labour that the U.S. positions were a basis for "serious dialogue." At first, Washington treated Begin's refusal to be itself a negotiating position, underestimating both Begin's outrage and his conviction that Camp David had indeed been abandoned. In the view of one Israeli analyst the U.S. positions "could shake the very compromise" on which Camp David was based— avoiding any prescription of final status in order to achieve a workable transition agreement that would improve relations among the parties.[16]

The immediate difficulty—the fatal difficulty—with the Reagan plan was its failure to produce the most effective form of pressure on Begin: an Arab party ready to negotiate. On September 9, five days after Israel rejected the plan, the Arab Summit at Fez reiterated long held positions incompatible with the American stand. By linking Lebanon and the West Bank, the U.S. had also given both Israel and Syria perverse incentives to stall over Lebanese withdrawal. Soon the U.S. was embroiled in drawn out negotiations with King Hussein, who in order to proceed needed a settlement freeze, PLO assent and later, as Syrian power revived, an international conference. (His negotiations with Arafat also fell victim to Syrian and Iraqi influence.) By the spring of 1983, Shultz was engaged

---

territories. See Statement of Secretary of State to U.S. House of Representatives Committee on Foreign Affairs, September 9, 1982, p. 8.

[16]See Lapidoth, *op. cit.*, p. 26. The Reagan proposals occasioned a battle of the commentaries. Alan J. Kreczko, Legal Advisor to Strauss and Linowitz, defended the initiative as consonant with the Camp David Accords, while Ruth Lapidoth, Legal Advisor to the Israeli negotiatiors, argued otherwise. See Alan J. Kreczko, "Support Reagan's Initiative," *Foreign Policy*, Winter 1982-83 and Ruth Lapidoth, *op. cit.*

instead in brokering the still-born Israel-Lebanon Peace Treaty and Special Negotiator Fairbanks had become a Special Ambassador to the Lebanese inter-party talks aimed at reconstituting the Lebanese Government.

SUMMING IT UP

Throughout the 1981-82 period the autonomy negotiations exhibited characteristics familiar to its earlier stages. Egyptian, American and Israeli positions reflected widely different concepts of autonomy; the peace treaty with Egypt retained its primacy; Jordanians and the Palestinians were still absent; and the press of other events in the area overtook the negotiations. Half a year had elapsed before a re-elected Menachem Begin, Anwar Sadat and the Reagan Administration could resume the work of Camp David where Jimmy Carter and Sol Linowitz left off. Begin and Sadat were not the same men they had been the year before; each was politically restricted and focused on other matters. The American official most committed to the Camp David Accords, Secretary of State Haig, was an increasingly isolated figure in an Administration not very enthusiastic about the Accords and not especially interested.

Then there was plain bad luck. Just when Begin and Sadat had resolved to finish the matter, Sadat was murdered. Haig's intention to press for agreement was diverted by a shared Egyptian and Israeli desire not to see the final withdrawal from Sinai burdened by an autonomy crisis. The position of Special Negotiator was revived to keep autonomy at least in motion if not in movement until a better moment. That moment may have come in the summer of 1982 but then the Lebanese War transformed the situation once more.

Palestinian and Jordanian objections to autonomy were based largely on the Palestinian demand for an independent state and Jordan's interest in the swift resumption of sovereign control over most, if not all, the territory lost in 1967. Both were heavily influenced by Syrian objections to a peace process that held little appeal for Damascus, by Saudi reticence and by Iraqi intimidation. Strategically, the Iran-Iraq war and Israel's defeat of both the PLO and Syria in Lebanon incapacitated the rejectionist front of Arabs opposed to Camp David. But the Israeli victory was flawed; both the PLO and Syria were able to recover, partly with Soviet help. Through the Reagan plan

America attempted to distance itself from Israel, still endorse Camp David and somehow attract the Jordanians to negotiations that would begin with autonomy. This proved both tactically and strategically inept and indeed replicated the earlier Carter experience, when the White House attempted to "sell" autonomy to the PLO and the other Arabs as a corridor to Arab sovereignty.

Essentially, the parties to the negotiations were able to agree on free elections, and on a Self-Governing Authority with a significant list of exclusive powers.[17] Conceivably there could have been some important shared powers if the Israeli proposal for development of future land and water had been taken up. A compromise on the size of the authority seemed within reach (more than Israel's 13 but less than Egypt's 80) and some other issues may have been amenable to American bridging proposals if they had been offered in a better negotiating context than the free-standing Reagan initiative. The five major areas of disagreement left at the end of the Linowitz period were still there in 1982, and the final American "stab" at a plan made in Washington simply aggravated the differences.

The negotiating record, however, does hold important implications for the future. These four points emerge clearly:

(1) Interim Agreements Are Not the Last Word: Attempts to "guarantee" the end game through an interim agreement will make even the interim step impossible. Self-Government (Autonomy) does not assure Palestinian national independence nor does it guarantee eventual Israeli sovereignty over the territory.

(2) The "Last Word" Will Still Intrude: there **are** long-term consequences flowing from different negotiating positions; the fear of those consequences will intrude even as interim steps are discussed.

(3) Outside Help Will Be Needed: Given the risks to be run by both Arabs and Israelis on issues such as security, land, water, settlements, and Jerusalem, outside help in reducing these risks and overcoming the obstacles will be necessary. The U.S. remains best suited to play the role of mediator but

---

[17]Reportedly, the working groups spent much time debating whether Israel's insistence that some of the autonomy's powers be subject to a negotiated "coordination and cooperation" with Israel seriously depleted real Palestinian authority. [See Appendix IX under POWERS, point 2]

other international support will also be needed both within the regime and out of it.

(4) **The Deal Must Work On Its Own Terms:** A larger peace process involving state-to-state negotiations can encourage an autonomy agreement but cannot be a substitute for an Israeli-Palestinian deal that works for both sides. Similarly, autonomy **can** facilitate state-to-state peace diplomacy (as it did for Egypt and Israel) but only if those states have independently decided to seek peace on sound bilateral foundations.

V FROM AUTONOMY TO SELF-GOVERNMENT

Following the failure of the Reagan Plan, autonomy was relegated to the archives until early 1988. For nearly five years a deadly stalemate prevailed in Middle East diplomacy. Badly bruised by its Lebanon experience, the Reagan Administration reduced its exposure to the Arab-Israeli conflict. Secretary Shultz, his faith in the Arabs shaken by Syrian and Saudi behavior in 1982-83, found better working relations with an Israeli government free of both Begin and Sharon—both casualties of the Lebanon disaster.

The Israeli National Unity Government of 1984-88 was formed to extricate Israel from Lebanon and to reform an economy nearly out of control. Peres and Shamir agreed to rotate the prime minister's post, each to serve two years, while the Defense Ministry was assigned to Rabin. The U.S., working with Prime Minister Peres, again tried to lure Jordan into a peace process in which autonomy would play a distinctly lesser role [See Appendix XII for the so-called Peres-Hussein Agreement]. These efforts were still-born and with Yitzhak Shamir's assumption of leadership, they ceased altogether.[1] Egypt continued to observe a "cold peace" with Israel and had lost interest in Palestinian autonomy.

---

[1] Also for naught were the attempts by the U.S., Jordan and Israel to stimulate economic development in the territories with international support. (These included the American "quality of life" program, the Jordanian Development Plan and Israel's call for resettlement of refugees, especially in Gaza.)

It was rather the Palestinians themselves who inadvertently revived the entire subject. As noted earlier, the diplomatic discussions on a Self-Governing Authority had never found a Palestinian interlocutor. But over the five years following the Reagan Plan the territories had not been still. Already in the early 1980s, the Israeli Military Government had had to assume the duties of the dismissed mayors while Sharon's brief experiment with the Village Leagues had further fractured the lines of administration. Especially following 1983, there had been a large influx of Israeli settlers, drawn less by ideology than by better living conditions—bedroom suburbs rather than pioneering settlements became the norm across the Green Line. Finally, the Palestinians themselves felt a steady encroachment of the Israeli bureaucracy, economy and society on their own lives. Dayan's strictures "to leave them alone" had been left behind.

Already in the summer of 1987, American officials had warned Israel that the territories were near-filled with explosive discontent. Following Israel's losses in Lebanon, the Palestinians seemed more assertive. Then in December of 1987 a traffic accident in Gaza touched off what became known as the *intifadah*—a broad-scale civilian rebellion against Israeli authority. Israel's reaction, slow and confused, was often brutal and highly divisive both within Israel and among Israel's friends abroad. The Israelis were not alone in being surprised by the *intifadah*. The PLO did not have control over the uprising nor were the aging members of Arafat's coteries numbered among its heroes. As for Jordan, Hussein did not think the *intifadah* would last and, when it did, he feared its impact on his own population.

THE SHULTZ INITIATIVE

In February 1988, as the *intifadah* raged, a number of Israeli officials were invited to Washington to discuss the Palestinian revolt.[2] Among them was Elyakim Rubinstein, a former close

---

[2]Palestinian leaders from the territories submitted a list of 14 demands to Shultz on January 14, 1988. While much of the political material was familiar, including the call for an international conference with the PLO in attendance, points 9-13 emphasized pragmatic issues of elections, taxation, land and water—all reminiscent of the Autonomy negotiations. [See Appendix XIII]

assistant to Moshe Dayan, who had also served as the Legal Advisor to the Israeli autonomy team in late 1981-82. Working with Charles Hill, Secretary of State Shultz's Executive Assistant and a veteran of the 1981-82 period, Rubinstein reviewed the autonomy plan, and the Israeli positions, including the idea of a shared control over the future development of land and water.

Later, after studying the autonomy "file" himself, Shultz became convinced that the concept held promise, but needed "repackaging." It was especially important in his view to shorten the time-frames both for reaching early agreements on a transition scheme and for commencing talks on the final status of the West Bank and Gaza. This was intended to reassure the Palestinians that autonomy would not be an open-ended "stall" by Israel. After a month of hectic planning and diplomacy, Shultz wrote both Shamir and King Hussein on March 4, 1988 with these proposals [See Appendix XIV]:

(1) Bilateral negotiations "for comprehensive peace providing for the security of all states in the region and for the legitimate rights of the Palestinian people" would be based on UN Security Council Resolutions 242 and 338.

(2) The bilateral Israeli talks with a Jordanian-Palestinian delegation would set a target for agreement within six months on "arrangements for a transitional period." Seven months after these discussions commenced, final status negotiations would begin. Most importantly, these latter negotiations would commence **before** the transition scheme was inaugurated or even agreed upon. This feature was known as the "interlock" between transition and final status talks. The transition period itself was shortened to three years.

(3) The United States would submit a draft agreement at the outset on transitional arrangements in order to speed up the negotiations.

(4) Finally, the bilateral negotiations would themselves be preceded by an international conference, with invitations presented by the UN Secretary General and attended by the five permanent members of the Security Council. The conference, however, could not impose or veto agreements. All participants had to renounce terrorism and support 242.

The Shultz plan tried to offer something for everybody: It attempted to attract Jordan through an international conference, protect Israel against the "gang-up" inherent in such a constellation, and exclude the PLO while attracting the Palestinians and Jordanians through the interlock feature of a rapid advance to final status negotiations. Probably, the "draft agreement" to be submitted by the U.S. was to be based on the Reagan bridging proposals of 1982. The entire scheme was to be propelled by the Israeli desire for transition and the Arab desire for final status, the timing of both more compressed than Camp David.

This was most ambitious, especially for an administration in its final year, and while it combined features attractive to each of the parties, it fell short of their respective minimum requirements. Washington still had no answer to Hussein's Syria problem and Syria had no interest in seeing a limited conference or an Israeli-Jordanian negotiation on its own. The PLO saw nothing in it at all. And the Israelis now saw the results crossing Shamir's red lines: a UN-sponsored conference and significant alterations to Begin's sacrosanct Camp David Accord on autonomy. As an alternative to a conference, Shamir suggested to Shultz that the U.S. and the USSR—under Gorbachev an increasingly promising source of Jewish immigration—"invite" the parties to bilateral negotiations.

An unexpected result of the U.S. effort was King Hussein's conclusion that he simply could do no further business with the PLO or the Palestinians while the *intifadah* raged on. Disappointed and angry at Arafat's denial of a Jordanian role, even as the PLO enjoyed a presence in Amman to monitor and coordinate the revolt, the King took a dramatic step. On July 31, 1988, he announced a cutting of legal and administrative ties to the West Bank, including the salaries Jordan had since 1967 paid to about 30 percent of the local Palestinian public bureaucracy. This harmed both the Jordanian and Palestinian economies far more than Hussein intended; there was a run on the Jordanian banks, and the dinar, still common currency in the West Bank, suffered a rapid devaluation. The King's move also signalled the U.S. that its concept of a joint delegation was no longer possible. By early fall, Shultz's plan had petered out.

The U.S. seemed resigned to stalemate in the Arab-Israeli conflict for some time to come, and Shultz gave a kind of valedictory address in September chiding all sides.[3] Then the Palestinians again changed the situation, this time through diplomacy. In November 1988, Arafat had declared a Palestinian State with himself as President. This was followed by the unthinkable. After secret exchanges through the Swedes and several false starts, Arafat at long last appeared to satisfy America's conditions for dialogue: recognition of Israel's right to exist; unconditional support of 242 and 338; and public renunciation of terrorism. Shultz announced that a U.S.-PLO dialogue would commence forthwith but specified that none of this indicated American acceptance of Arafat's two state solution.[4]

THE SHAMIR-RABIN PEACE PLAN: AUTONOMY BECOMES SELF-RULE

As a consequence of both the PLO's declaration and the *intifadah*, the Israeli government found itself in early 1989 at the nadir of its diplomatic fortunes. Elections in November 1988 had given the Likud a margin over Labour but not enough to rule except in coalition with fringe parties pressing drastic demands. Another national unity government had been formed, this one built around Shamir as Prime Minister while Peres took the Finance post. Rabin, who remained as Defense Minister, had been carrying out the controversial attempt to suppress the *intifadah* by force, which led to highly publicized scenes of Israeli soldiers beating young Palestinian stone-throwers. The course of events convinced him that Israel needed a combined military-diplomatic offensive to turn the mounting *intifadah*-PLO tide.

This became all the more necessary because there was a new administration in Washington. The President, George Bush, and his Secretary of State, James A. Baker III, did not enjoy the same repute as Reagan and Shultz when it came to

---

[3]The Secretary of State spoke to the annual policy conference of The Washington Institute for Near East Policy. For text see *Proceedings of Middle East Diplomacy: The Wye Plantation Speech*, (Washington, D.C.: The Washington Institute for Near East Policy, 1988).

[4]For the Arafat declaration and Shultz's response, see *Journal of Palestine Studies* Vol. 18 (3), Spring 1989, p. 161 and State Department Briefing, December 14, 1988, from Federal News Service.

dealing with Israel. Moreover, there were enormous changes afoot in Europe and the Soviet Union that would, within two years of Bush's inauguration, end the Cold War, reunite Germany and terminate Moscow's control of Eastern Europe. Israel would have to make her case under circumstances very different than those prevalent earlier in the decade.

Finally, on April 6, 1989, while visiting the White House, Shamir took the initiative. His new plan, elaborated in much greater detail by the Cabinet five weeks later, consisted of four parts: (1) a warming of the cold Egyptian-Israeli peace to fulfill Camp David's objectives as the cornerstone of peace; (2) state-to-state negotiations for a comprehensive settlement; (3) an international effort to resolve the refugee problem in Judea, Samaria and Gaza; (4) free and democratic elections "in an atmosphere devoid of violence, threats and terror" to elect representatives from the territories "to conduct negotiations for a transitional period of self-rule." A later stage would bring negotiations for a permanent solution in which "all the proposed options for an agreed settlement will be examined." All of these points were to be pursued simultaneously. [See Appendix XV for text]

Israel's detailed explanations for the fourth point did indeed put the plan squarely in the stream of earlier conceptions of autonomy. It "restored" the Camp David formula instead of the Shultz "interlock": five years of transition, with final status talks to begin "no later" than year three. This was not new. But the Israeli emphasis on electing Palestinian representatives and dealing with them as an independent group did break new ground. Jordan and Egypt would be "invited" only if they wished to participate in transitional negotiations. For the first time Israel also publicly limited its exclusive powers during the transition to security, foreign affairs and jurisdiction over the Israeli citizens living in the territories. And Israel also specified that elections be "regional" rather than municipal or local.

Two other interesting linkages were drawn by Shamir and the official Israeli commentary on the plan. First, Shamir stressed that self-rule would be much less risky in 1989 than it might have been in 1979 because there were now 80,000

Jewish settlers.[5] The second linkage concerned the impact of the peace between Israel and the Arab states on the negotiations over the territories' **final** status: "its realization [full peace]—or non-realization—will determine what kind of concessions Israel will (or will not) be able to offer the Palestinian Arabs when the future political status of Judea, Samaria and the Gaza District will come up for discussion."[6]

There was one notable omission from the Israeli initiative. Nowhere, not in the Cabinet communique, not in Shamir's speech, and not in official commentary does the word "autonomy" appear. Instead, "self-rule" becomes the Israeli term of choice.

In terms of Israel's decade-old approach to the Palestinian issue, these were very forward proposals and they immediately achieved their first objective of appealing to Washington. But would they appeal to the Arabs? Secretary of State Baker soon concluded that the key to movement was point four, the elections. And here there was a catch: the "selection" before the "election." Who would become the Palestinian interlocutors from the territories with whom Israel could reach agreement on election procedures? How would they be chosen? Rabin preferred ambiguity: "We'll know them when we see them."[7] Shamir suggested that the U.S. and Egypt could be helpful in selecting the list.[8] The PLO, of course, would be excluded.

Baker found, however, that Palestinian (and Egyptian) support depended on an "outsider" and an Arab from East Jerusalem being included as part of the delegation. The reader who has toiled this far will recognize immediately the Palestinian purpose of reinserting the PLO's constituency from

---

[5]English translation of Knesset statement, May 17, 1989, under imprint of the Israeli Embassy, Washington D.C. as communicated by Shamir's media advisor and as delivered on IDF radio.

[6]Background Paper, Embassy of Israel Washington D.C., "Commentary and Analysis," Jerusalem, May 14, 1989.

[7]Comment to The Washington Institute for Near East Policy Study Group, June 1989.

[8]Comment to The Washington Institute for Near East Policy Study Group, June 1989.

"outside" the territories on the one hand and asserting its claim to Jerusalem on the other. Eventually, in October 1989, Baker advanced a five-point framework for an Israeli-Palestinian "dialogue" in Cairo to be preceded by a U.S.-Israeli-Egyptian meeting in Washington which would agree on a list and an agenda.[9] The Israeli Cabinet accepted this proposal along with six(!) assumptions about it on November 5.[10] A month later, on December 6, Egypt accepted as well, attaching a PLO response for Baker and trumping the six Israeli assumptions with even more of its own.[11]

The path now seemed open to possible compromises on the main sticking points over the Palestinian list. The U.S. proposed that the parties accept Palestinians who were prepared to support the two phase (transitional/final status) process suggested by Israel and who otherwise subscribed to UN Resolutions 242, 338 and anti-terrorism. The Americans still hoped to satisfy the Palestinian requirements by selecting a "deportee"—a Palestinian expelled from the territories for anti-Israel activities but who, even under Israeli law, had a residual right to return. As for Jerusalem, the solution might be to choose a dual addressee: a candidate with two residences, one outside the city.

These were exercises in parallax diplomacy. Viewed from one side they offered the PLO and the West Bankers the presence they demanded; viewed from the Israeli side, these Palestinian interlocutors could still plausibly be regarded as "inhabitants" of the territories, neither PLO nor Jerusalemite. But the parties had to want to see it that way.

---

[9]Among other items, Baker's points also stated U.S. "understandings" that Israel would attend only if a "satisfactory" list of Palestinians "worked out." See *Mideast Mirror*, December 7, 1989, for texts of U.S., Israeli and Egyptian "points."

[10]These included Israel's insistance on negotiating only with acceptable residents of the West Bank and Gaza, exclusion of the PLO, and the agenda to be Palestinian elections in the framework of Israel's peace proposal.

[11]In early September, Egypt had published a ten-point plan differing with the Israeli election proposal and insisting that Israel accept, among other items, an end to settlement activities, the exchange of land for peace and East Jerusalem Arab participation in the elections. See *Mideast Mirror, op.cit.*

Before the Americans could be sure of that, and before the Washington meeting could be held, there was a dramatic interlude as events elsewhere captured the world's attention. The Berlin Wall came down. Not long thereafter, the process of German reunification began as the East German regime rapidly collapsed. A general European crisis seemed at hand.

When the U.S. resumed its push in early 1990, parallax diplomacy came close but still fell short. Weakened by opposition in his own party and under severe public pressure from both the United States and his Labour Party partner, Shamir lost the Unity Government on March 15, 1990, rather than accept the American proposals. In the sensational maneuvers that always attend the formation of an Israeli government, Shamir bested Peres once more, managing to form a new coalition well to the political right. Shamir's ally Moshe Arens became Defense Minister while the three Likud politicians most opposed to the U.S. proposals were given important offices: David Levy, new to international affairs, became Foreign Minister; Yitzhak Moda'i took Finance; and Ariel Sharon was assigned to run what had become the new Government's highest priority, creating housing for the flood of Soviet immigrants.

THE GULF WAR AND ITS AFTERMATH: "INTERIM SELF-GOVERNMENT"

There the matter might have remained for some time if not for Iraq's seizure of Kuwait and Saddam Hussein's attempt to link the Arab-Israeli conflict to his own aggression in the Gulf. At the time, this tactic earned Saddam the enthusiastic support of the PLO and the Palestinians living on both sides of the Jordan River, contributing heavily to King Hussein's own "tilt" toward the Iraqis. It did not touch off popular uprisings elsewhere, instead revolting both the Israelis and the former Palestinian strongholds of support amongst the Gulf Sheikhdoms—especially Saudi Arabia.

While the U.S. resisted this linkage, President Bush made clear on more than one occasion, including in his speech to the United Nations on October 1, 1990, that once the crisis was resolved he would resume a push for Arab-Israeli peace. On March 6, 1991, after announcing the victory over Iraq, Bush also told the Congress that "the time has come to end the Arab-

Israeli conflict" on the basis of security, land for peace and legitimate Palestinian rights. Within two weeks of the war, Secretary of State Baker was sent out to "catalyze" the dormant peace process.

After an exhausting series of visits, Baker was able to report a narrowing of differences on a proposal to convene a "regional" peace conference. Almost unnoticed in the controversies over the conference procedures was Baker's statement to a House subcommittee on May 22 that he found "agreement that the negotiations between Israel and the Palestinians would proceed in phases, with talks on interim self-government preceding negotiations over the permanent status of the Occupied Territories" [See Appendix XVI]. Then on May 31, President Bush wrote the leaders of Egypt, Israel, Jordan and Syria asking them to accept the U.S. approach to a conference: it should be a ceremonial prelude to bilateral negotiations based on 242 and 338; the UN should be represented by a mute observer; European and Gulf Council observers would also be present; and it could not be reconvened without mutual consent.

A month later, Prime Minister Shamir rejected the President's ideas, but Syria's surprise acceptance of the conference format on July 14, 1991 soon led to an Israeli reversal. As it turned out, the Israelis were far more interested in the problem of Palestinian representation and on that issue, the Gulf War had brought about a considerable change. The Likud government had discovered the virtues of King Hussein, even as a buffer publicly sympathetic to Iraq. Though the King's performance had put him and Jordan in bad odour with the victors, Shamir was arguing that nonetheless the King had a crucial role to play: the senior Arab partner of the Palestinians. Israel therefore insisted that the Palestinians be part of a Jordanian delegation—so long as neither PLO figures nor an East Jerusalemite were on it.

The new Israeli position was actually an old one, reverting to the original Camp David approach. In the first stage of negotiations over an interim agreement Palestinians were to be part of the Egyptian and Jordanian delegations, not their own group. Only **after** an autonomy agreement had been reached would elections for a Self-Governing Authority legitimize the Palestinians on their own. Shamir's 1989 plan had reversed this sequence, treating the Palestinians as a political force independently of the Arab states—an oblique testimony to the achievement of the *intifadah*. But now the gains of the *intifadah* had been wiped out in the Palestinians' fatal alliance with Saddam. Shamir was thus able to insist on Palestinian representation that excluded PLO "outsiders" and Jerusalem "insiders"—the very proposals that had broken his government the year before—in the context of a Jordanian delegation.

On October 17, 1991, Secretary Baker and Soviet Foreign Minister Boris Pankin were able to announce from Jerusalem that a peace conference would be held in Madrid on October 30. The Palestinians would be participating as members of a joint delegation with Jordan. Two days later, on October 19, Israel formally agreed to attend the conference.

This turn of events ratified the astonishing reversal of Palestinian political fortunes and an equally astonishing revival of the interim "self-government" concept. The decade of the eighties had begun with the most vigorous Palestinian rejections of autonomy. As the years passed, the PLO's cause grew stronger, reaching its apogee in 1988 when the *intifadah* and Arafat's statements earned it a dialogue with the U.S. But not twenty-four months later, the tide sweeping toward Palestinian statehood had crested and crashed, leaving upon the diplomatic sands the shards of the disastrous Iraqi alliance. The Palestinians, even to be part of a negotiation, were now face to face with "self-government" as the best they would get, shorn of even symbolic expressions of their national aspirations or their claim to Jerusalem. In their long struggle to emerge as an independent actor, the Palestinians had now but a single part to play: as members of a joint delegation with Jordan to negotiate not independence but Self-Government (Autonomy).

VI AMERICAN POLICY AND PALESTINIAN SELF-GOVERNMENT

The United States is now poised to help Israel, Jordan and the Palestinians take up Palestinian Self-Government (Autonomy) for the West Bank and Gaza, under far more favorable circumstances than ever before. First, unlike the 1979-82 period, there is no substantial Arab Rejectionist Front, nor a Soviet superpower willing to arm it. Those Arabs who reject peace negotiations are either defeated or weak and they cannot look to external powers for effective support. Second, American mediation—Washington's words of support or opposition—will carry very great weight. After the victory over Iraq and the collapse of the Soviet Union, more than ever before there is no alternative to the United States as the sole outside power best able to reduce the risks and enlarge the rewards in reaching agrement. Third and most important, the local parties have persuasive reasons to seek a change in the status quo.

Israel's most dangerous enemies are at bay but the country needs economic and political reforms and faces a huge burden of new immigration; simultaneously, tensions between Arabs and Jews are worse than ever; and external pressures for a resolution of the conflict are mounting. The Palestinians are suffering a season of reverses: a fresh flood of refugees from the Gulf, the end of broad Arab support for their cause, little to show for the heavy casualties of the *intifadah*, and a mounting Israeli settler population in their midst. And Jordan, itself isolated from its traditional friends by its position during the

Gulf War, is more than ever a state whose destiny is determined by the ebb and flow of the Palestinian issue.

In short, the parties badly need a change towards peace, international politics favor it, and the United States is well placed to encourage it.

Enthusiasm in this case, however, needs the counsel of both experience from past peacemaking and a keen sense of what Palestinian Self-Government can and cannot do to resolve the Arab-Israeli conflict.

LESSONS FROM THE PAST[1]

First, the United States should sustain a certain *balance* in its relationships to the local protagonists. The U.S. is an ally of Israel committed to its security but also vitally interested in good relations with the Arabs and eager for a settlement of the draining conflict between the two. American policy has usually operated in this context and any substantial change— e.g., the end of alliance with Israel, loss of interest in the Arabs or passivity about the conflict—will convince one or another of the parties that Washington is dangerous to its vital interests. The resulting friction will force the U.S. either to impose a settlement or to abandon the quest—neither a recipe for an enduring peace.

Second, the United States should encourage the parties to find and build on common interests. American diplomacy has been able to "broker" lasting deals only between parties who really wanted to make them. By "broker" I mean that rather than creating a U.S. plan to force on the parties, the U.S. instead reinforced common interests by reducing the risks for Israel and its Arab negotiating partner so that they could agree on their own basic terms. In contrast, every attempt to put forward an American plan prematurely has relieved the regional powers of having to do anything except resist—a famous Middle Eastern art form. There is a place for American advocacy, but only when the parties have come sufficiently close to each other that a "bridging" proposal originated by Washington is both practical and clearly desired.

---

[1]This portion draws partly on Kenneth W. Stein and Samuel W. Lewis, *Making Peace Among Arabs and Israelis: Lessons from Fifty Years of Negotiating Experience,* (Washington, D.C.: United States Institute of Peace, 1991).

Third, while the USSR may be co-chairman of a conference and the European states will continue to play some role, they are not alternatives to the U.S., although their actions could harm American efforts. Only the United States has sufficient clout and credibility with all sides to ease their very difficult choices. And upon the United States falls the task of keeping the other political hounds either at bay or making the right sounds: keeping the signals straight and the atmosphere conducive to progress.

Fourth, the United States should be continually involved. While direct talks are an important psychological breakthrough, especially for Israel, they do not guarantee success. If the Egyptian-Israeli negotiations are any guide, then the parties will be loathe to make open concessions to each other and in any event they will look to the U.S. to reduce their risks when they do. And for the United States, the most critical dimension of this new round of diplomacy will be to evoke movement by the parties toward each other based on their overlapping interests, rather than what they imagine will play in Washington.

Fifth, there is no substitute for the President. The time-consuming twists and turns of Arab-Israeli negotiations also raise questions about the bureaucratics of the American approach: how much time ought to be spent and who should spend it? What are the respective roles of working experts, the Secretary of State, the President, and a Special Negotiator—if any? A decade and a half of experience yields these clues:

A strong working group is indispensable not only to pave the way and clean up the debris but to "signal" a troubling state of play or an opportunity to those higher up.

The Secretary of State or a high-level personal representative (Special Negotiator) of either the Secretary or the White House can effectively deal with 90 percent of the issues providing that the official is regarded by the parties as competent, empathetic (if not sympathetic) and authoritative, i.e., his position is likely to be upheld by higher authority.

Nonetheless the most important final compromises will require direct presidential intervention. When the parties are ready to take the final risk, they will want the President to be holding their hands as they leap—and they will want him to leap with them.

With these points in mind, the two questions posed at the outset of this study should now be answered. First, will Self-Government (Autonomy) solve the Palestinian problem or at least put it on the road to solution? The answer is that Self-Government cannot solve the Palestinian problem immediately, but properly conceived it is a vital step forward that will contribute eventually to a solution. Second, how should the United States help to bring it about? The answer is that Washington can use its special influence to broker a direct Israeli-Palestinian-Jordanian negotiation that builds on their common interest and reduces their risks, especially in the crucial areas of resources and military security.

THE PALESTINIAN PROBLEM AND THE POLITICS OF CONSENT

If Palestinian Self-Government is to play a significant role in resolving the Arab-Israeli conflict then it must be based on a careful understanding of that much abused phrase, the "Palestinian Problem." The problem can be stated precisely in geopolitical terms: who shall rule, Arab or Jew, over the territory defined after World War I as the "British Mandate for Palestine"? History's answer since 1921 has been Hashemite rule over the East Bank of the Jordan; after 1948, Israeli rule over part of the area west of the river, with Egypt and Jordan ruling over the rest; and, after 1967, Israeli control over all of western Palestine between the river and the sea while Jordan continues its control over the East Bank.

Israel and Hashemite Jordan might have composed their quarrel some time ago if their interests alone were at stake. Even under the so-called state of war, various Israeli governments and Jordanian monarchs have had amicable though unofficial relations, despite their clashes in 1948 and 1967. But they are not the only claimants to Palestine.

There live throughout the original mandate territory Arabs who consider themselves to be "Palestinians," that is, neither Jordanians nor Israelis.[2] Some are Jordanian citizens (half or more of the East Bank population) and some are Israeli citizens

---

[2]Population figures are drawn from "Palestinian Projections for 16 Countries/Areas of the World: 1990 to 2010." Washington D.C.: U.S. Bureau of the Census, September 1990-March 1991, unpublished.

(ten percent). A large group, a million and a half, live in the areas known as the West Bank and Gaza, hold Jordanian passports or are stateless refugees under Israeli military government. These and about 3.5 to 4 million living around the Middle East, and elsewhere, see themselves as either the rightful rulers of all of Palestine on both banks; or as the rightful rulers of all of western Palestine (Israel but not Jordan). More recently the Palestinians have tried to define their first claim as a right to the areas captured by Israel in the Six-Day War of 1967.

Thus, the historical issue of "who shall rule Palestine" has developed into the current question: "Should there be another Arab sovereignty—Palestinian sovereignty—over the areas occupied by Israel since 1967"?

Israel's answer has been "no" on the grounds of security alone, reinforced by Israel's own historical claims. But Israel for various reasons has never extended its domestic law into what the Israelis call Judea, Samaria and the Gaza District (except for Jerusalem). An Israeli government that did so would face enormous foreign and domestic opposition. The resulting state would certainly have a smaller Jewish majority, the new Soviet Jewish immigrants notwithstanding, and its future as a Jewish state would be questionable.

Jordan's answer has been "yes" if the independent Arab Palestine promptly joined in some sort of political union with it. But Jordanian rule over the West Bank between 1948 to 1967 was widely resented by the Palestinians, and the monarchy fought a bitter civil war against the PLO in 1970. Despite two major efforts in the 1980s, King Hussein and Yasser Arafat failed to agree on their precise relationship before entering a negotiation as a joint delegation. And Israel has refused a territorial redivision along any lines that would interest Jordan to go it alone without the Palestinians.

Finally, the Palestinian answer has been "yes" to "Filastin," an independent Palestinian state, on the grounds of their own right to self-determination and security. But the Palestinians have failed to convince Israel (and others) that their "two-state" solution would not threaten Israeli security. To the contrary: both the *intifadah* and the widespread and vocal Palestinian support for Iraqi missile attacks on Israel have convinced many that their aspiration is the destruction of the

Jewish state entirely, for which purpose the two-state solution is a stepping stone.

This mutual deadlock of competing and incompatible aspirations gives the Arab-Israeli conflict its special quality of bitter paralysis. Politics, however, is not only about aspirations: what people **want**. It is also about consent: what people will **accept**—even at some cost to their ideals—because there exists an overriding interest to do so.

The overriding interest in this case is not what Self-Government will do to fix the final status but what it can do to get beyond the terrors of the status quo. It should be clear from the outset that Self-Government (Autonomy) for the Palestinians cannot satisfy the ultimate aspirations of any of the parties. By definition, Self-Government (Autonomy) is a concept of limits. A self-governing authority will not be a full fledged international citizen—a state. Nor will it be a domesticated animal, that is, fully part of another state's laws. Those who aspire to extend, reclaim, or establish sovereignty over the areas in question will never find complete satisfaction in Self-Government.

Equally futile will be any attempt to define Self-Government (Autonomy) according to immaculate concepts of international law. In fact, the virtue of the concept is precisely its flexibility, depending on political requirements. It should come as no surprise to learn, as one eminent jurist long ago concluded, that "on no subject of international law has there been so much loose writing and nebulous speculation . . . "[3]

No doubt this author will add (or has already added!) his portion to the received body of loose writing and nebulous speculation. But if Self-Government is deficient, as judged against the respective ideals of Israel, Jordan and the Palestinians (and of international legal clarity), it is no more deficient than the status quo. None of the parties contesting control over the West Bank and Gaza are going to achieve their ideals in the foreseeable future. The issue therefore is not

---

[3]John Chipman Grey, *The Nature and Sources of the Law* (1909), quoted in "The Concept of Autonomy in International Law" Hurst Hannum and Richard B. Lillich, in Yoram Dinstein, ed., *Models of Autonomy* (New Brunswick: Transaction Books, 1981), p. 215. Hannum and Lillich produced a two-volume study for the Department of State in 1979-80 on "The Theory and Practice of Governmental Autonomy."

whether Self-Government achieves an ideal but rather, whether it meets the practical test for which the parties will give their consent: is it better than the status quo?

That test must first be passed with the Palestinians. They are the weakest party, the party furthest from the ideal and by far suffering the most from the status quo. Over 1000, mostly young, Palestinians have lost their lives in the four-year rebellion against Israeli rule (the *intifadah*). Their economy has been wrecked by the *intifadah* and the sudden impoverishment or dislocation of prosperous Gulf exile communities. Palestinian support for Iraq in the Gulf War also dashed whatever support they had in Israeli political movements such as "Peace Now." And, of course, the Israeli settler population continues to grow. Yet for these very reasons they have the most to gain from Self-Government and the most to lose should negotiations fail. Palestinian consent, however, will require a new dawning of pragmatic politics.

The emotional barriers should not be underestimated. The Palestinians believe that they were turned from a majority to a minority in their own country in less than a man's lifetime; that their Arab brothers failed to rescue them and often exploited their misery; and that the United States in particular has allowed Israel to deny them the most elementary national and human rights. This sense of historic wrong and oppression has only been deepened by recent events. For them the Gulf War was an opportunity to threaten Israel militarily and to protest what they regarded as a double-standard, yet it resulted in the devastation of the Palestinian community in Kuwait, a further alienation from Western sympathies and widespread loss of support throughout the Gulf—the great financial pillar of the Palestinian struggle.

While unified in their resentment, the Palestinians have found political unity elusive. Violent personal rivalries and shifting alliances have marked their political history, manipulated throughout by various Arab states: Egypt, Syria, Iraq, Saudi Arabia, Jordan have each attempted to capture either part or all of the Palestinian cause for their own purposes.[4] The Palestinians are also divided by their location: the "insiders,"

---

[4]In fact, the creation of the PLO in 1964 was largely an attempt by then Egyptian President Gamal Abdul Nasser to solidify Palestinian nationalists under his patronage.

those under Israeli military rule in the West Bank and Gaza, and the "outsiders," the Palestinian exiles and emigres scattered around the Middle East and elsewhere. The "insiders" have been more pragmatic if by pragmatism is meant accommodation to the fact of Israeli rule. Their particular grievances—except for Jerusalem—are not territorial but political: who rules and how it is done. Most of the Gazans, however, share with the "outside" Palestinian diaspora a territorial claim to pre-1967 Israel that cannot be settled by Palestinian Self-Government in the post-1967 West Bank.

Except for a few occasions when the "insiders" got their way on tactical issues, such as municipal elections in 1976, the PLO and its factions gave the Palestinians under occupation what leadership they had until late 1987. But the *intifadah* was purely a product of the "inside" and raised the issue of whether those bearing the heaviest burden of the struggle should not also assume more of a role in the diplomacy that might end or at least ease the conflict. And the "insiders," including a new group empowered either by their generalship of the *intifadah* or their espousal of Islamic purity, did make a mark, and not only in the war of images and nerves. Thus, resistance to the Israelis in Gaza, where the Islamic Hamas Party is strongest, has led Israel to diminish if not relinquish its presence rather than completely quash the rebellion. And in the U.S.-sponsored diplomacy of 1989, which broke down over Palestinian representation, the PLO seemed prepared to let the insiders take the initial steps.

Indeed Shamir's elections proposal stimulated a lively debate among Palestinians over a Palestinian "initiative," not to negotiate autonomy but to reform the PLO. This polemic was given additional force after the Gulf War. While Iraq's cause had been popular in the territories, the PLO's handling of the situation was regarded as disastrous, bolstering the case for "new blood" and "new concepts." One idea hotly discussed was to run elections that would enlarge the role of "insiders" in the Palestine National Council, to be followed by an agreement with Jordan on confederation, even before negotiating with Israel.[5] Israel presumably would use the

---

[5] See Radi Jerrai in *Al Fajr* (an English-language Palestinian weekly published in Jerusalem), April 1, 1991, p. 4. See also *Al Fajr* April 8, 22 and 28, 1991. This paper lists its contributors' Israeli jail records as proof of their political credentials.

election device as a way to come to terms with legitimate Palestinian representatives, even if they were members of the PLO.[6] These are all attempts to reshape the Palestinian direction in the wake of a war grievously disappointing to those hoping for a national redemption by force or divine intervention. And they reflect the desire of those who would negotiate to do so without a personally dangerous rejection of the defiant symbol of Palestinian unity—Yasser Arafat, since November 15, 1988, self-declared President of the State of Filastin (Palestine).

While, in the absence of any alternative, the "insiders" and those advocating the diplomatic route are bound to gain strength in one way or another, Palestinians inclined to negotiate face great personal and collective risks. A Palestinian Rejectionist Front, whether *intifadist*, Islamicist or terrorist in origin, will threaten any delegation.[7] Self-Government for the West Bank and Gaza inherently emphasizes the "inside" over the "outside." And the Palestinians have reason to fear that the Arab states, once they are into the diplomacy, will reach their own deals with Israel, leaving the Palestinians without leverage and without prospects.

Yet even as those Palestinians who want a diplomatic process argue their need for a promise of self-determination and a visible role for the "outsiders" (the PLO), there is a growing recognition that Self-Government may be the only practical way to advance. De facto chief "inside" interlocutor Faisal Husseini's account of one of his meetings with U.S. Secretary of State James Baker illustrates the point: " . . . James Baker said to us, 'You will obtain a little less than a state and more than autonomy.' We replied, 'We don't want to exchange slogans, but to discuss the substance. This entity you refer to, will it be able to apply the right of return for the Palestinians scattered and persecuted around the world? If so, we can talk' . . . "[8] Compared with Begin's original proposal

---

[6]See Daoud Kuttab, *The Washington Post*, April 16, 1989.

[7]The leadership of the *intifadah* itself has passed from a Unified National Command composed of local grassroots leaders, to bands of increasingly violent youths, unanswerable to virtually any authority.

[8]Interview, *Journal of Palestine Studies*, Volume XX, No. 4, Summer 1991, p. 107.

(point 21) for a joint Israeli-Palestinian-Jordanian Committee to regulate the return of refugees to the territories, one can see the makings of a practical negotiation over even this sensitive issue.

There is a developing record of possible Palestinian positions on the details of Self-Government. As noted earlier, an extensive survey was done by one researcher immediately after Camp David. More recently a full scale peace plan was published by Palestinian lawyer and journalist Talal Abu Afifeh (al-Safi), reportedly a Fatah activist.[9] From these plans reported in the Palestinian media one can assemble a Palestinian position on "interim self-government":

• The goal of transition is to facilitate the final status of Palestinian independence.

• The PLO must have a role so that insider-outsider unity can be sustained.

• Strict limitations must be placed on Israel's military movement.

• Palestinians must enjoy total control over land, water and resources.

• Israeli settlement activity should be frozen either before negotiations begin or certainly when the transition period starts; and they should eventually be removed or subject to Palestinian authority.

• Provisions must be made for the return of refugees to the self-governing territory

• East Jerusalem must be included as the projected capital of the Palestinian entity—physically undivided but politically separate.[10]

• The interim stages agreement must be under International or UN supervision including (if requested) a UN civilian and military presence.

• And some Palestinian-Jordanian political accord, usually called a "Confederation," would be reached.

---

[9]Dr. Ann Lesch, *Journal of Palestinine Studies*, Volume IX, No. 3, Spring 1980, pp.189-91, and Talal Abu Afifeh (al-Safi) in *Al-Fajr*, May 13, 1991. Al-Safi's credentials include numerous arrests for security felonies, including two years in jail for leading a Fatah group.

[10]Talal Abu Afifeh (al-Safi) suggests a UN role over East Jerusalem as an alternative to exclusive Palestinian control.

Many of these positions, of course, contradict both the Israeli and American concept that the interim agreement ought not determine in advance the outcome of final status negotiations. Like the Egyptian model circa 1980, the Palestinian sources see the interim Self-Government as a state in swaddling clothes, the passage of time serving largely to extend Palestinian control and remove the Israeli presence until an independent state linked to Jordan emerges in full sovereignty. Even if the Palestinians fail to obtain full scale assurances of this outcome before negotiations, they can be expected to judge each detail by whether it contributes to impending statehood. [See Appendix XVII for selected Palestinian quotes on Self-Government]

This approach may satisfy Palestinian ideals, but it suffers otherwise from severe defects. It will be forestalled by both Israel and the United States—perhaps also by Jordan—if the meaning of confederation is not clarified. It will accentuate the shortcomings of every agreement the Palestinians do reach by putting any attempt at Self-Government to the test of statehood—which, as argued earlier, by definition, it cannot pass.

Thus, if a Palestinian strategy for Self-Government is to succeed, more pragmatic goals must inform the Palestinian effort:

• getting rid of the military government and its intrusions;

• gaining some control over land, water and resources;

• improving the economy of the area so that it can "absorb" both the "inside" refugees and make a start on the most destitute of the outsiders;

• establishing secure and democratic institutions.

These are tall orders in themselves. They do not guarantee a state but they are certainly necessary building blocks to the further political development of the Palestinians. And at a minimum they will make it more difficult than ever for Israel to annex or absorb the territories. Palestinian Self-Government offers a potential solution to what Edward Said defined as his people's most pressing dilemma: " . . . a national movement that despite its many achievements . . . has not discovered a method for stopping or containing the relentless Israeli attempt to take over more and more Palestinian (as well as other Arab) territory."[11]

THE JORDANIAN OPTION REVISITED

The next test for consent is Jordan, containing a population more than half of whom are considered to be Palestinians. While the Palestinian nationalists have long conceived of Jordan as a necessary backdrop, ally and potential confederate, they have never been able to reach an enduring satisfactory relationship with its Hashemite rulers. From 1948 to 1967, when King Abdullah and later King Hussein held the upper hand in the West Bank, the Palestinians were kept firmly in second political place, although individuals were allowed high positions in the Court and Royal Administration. Beginning in 1968, the reborn PLO run by Arafat almost took over Jordan and a savage civil war ensued, culminating in Jordan's violent expulsion of the PLO in September 1970. The PLO's later disaster in Lebanon and subsequent deadly quarrel with Syria gave King Hussein an opening to reassert his leadership, but neither in 1982-83 nor later in 1985 could the King and Arafat agree on a lasting political *modus vivendi* for negotiations. Finally in 1988, Jordan officially "withdrew" from the Palestinian scene as the *intifadah* strengthened the PLO's hand.

Now both parties find themselves forced to work together on a joint delegation to peace talks and joint negotiations on Self-Government (Autonomy), a turn of events neither sought nor expected. The outcome will depend heavily on Jordan's own view of the virtues of Palestinian Self-Government.

King Hussein, unlike Yasser Arafat, has staged an astonishing recovery from the Gulf War during which his "tilt" toward Iraq appeared to cost him vital international support. By avoiding the twin disasters of either civil war (by adopting an anti-Iraq posture) or becoming a combatant (by attacking Israel) the King achieved a political feat unique even by Middle East standards: he became simultaneously popular with both the Palestinians and with Israel's Likud government. Now, as the designated "senior" partner of the Palestinians, his crucial role reaffirmed by Israel, Hussein is well on the way to

---

[11] Edward Said, "Reflections on Twenty Years of Palestinian History," *Journal of Palestine Studies*, Volume XX, No. 4, Summer 1991, p. 5.

shedding the discredited mufti of Saddam's ally for the more familiar cloak of Arab moderate.

These astonishing events, however, do not speak directly to Jordan's real interest and probable behavior when it comes to Palestinian Self-Government. The simple answer is that Jordan must have a role. The King cannot ignore the attachments of his Palestinian subjects, yet he cannot allow those attachments alone to determine his policy. Hussein's own concept of his dynasty's historic destiny is balanced against his justly famed instinct for survival.

It may be fashionable to pit the Palestinian nationalists as the antithesis of a bedouin-influenced monarchy, but Hussein actually regards himself as the supreme nationalist.[12] His family's role in the Arab Revolt is a legacy that qualifies Hussein—in his own eyes—to be in the vanguard of those who cherish Arab political independence and dignity. As a descendant of the Prophet, and inheritor of the title *Sherif*, the King will never take second place to the Islamists, although he does not press upon his subjects the dogmas of religion.

This being said, Hussein has throughout his career manifested a healthy respect for popular opinion, especially Palestinian. A large part of his population is tied by kinship, culture and history to the other side of the river; their causes and passions have involved him in civil war and war with Israel, and more recently made it impossible for him to openly side with the West in the Gulf crisis.

Another significant constant with which the King must reckon is Jordan's poverty. Jordan's lack of natural resources and indigenous wealth contribute to its regional vulnerability, and its immediate neighbors are all more powerful militarily than Jordan can ever be. Even worse, each could be suspected of harboring ambitions for Jordan—seen from Jerusalem as an extension of the Land of Israel, seen from Damascus as part of historic Greater Syria and seen from Saudi Arabia as a natural extension of the *Hijaz*. As a result, the King has always sought allies from outside the region both to survive and to prosper.

---

[12]See Uriel Dann, *The Survival Strategy of King Hussein In Historical Perspective*, (Forthcoming from The Washington Institute), and Hussein's own autobiography, *Uneasy Lies the Head*, (London: Heinemann, 1962).

Given its East Bank (i.e. non-Palestinian) power structure, loyal Bedouin army and a ruler keenly aware of the country's geopolitical vulnerability, Jordan could ill afford the extreme politics of the Palestinians. More than most of the Arab rulers who brought the catastrophe of 1967, Hussein was guilty in Palestinian eyes of having failed to protect them. Thereafter, Jordan posed as the power best able to recover the lost territories, but was never able to get the "goods" in the form of an acceptable Israeli territorial withdrawal or to "deliver" them in the form of Palestinian acquiescence to Jordan's senior role. The Palestinians know and Hussein knows that while occasionally he will be **with** them, Hashemite Jordan will never be **of** them. The King's survival (and Jordan's) depends on his control or containment of the Palestinians, not becoming an instrument of their cause.

This basic fissure at the core of Jordanian-Palestinian relations has made it impossible for Jordan and the PLO to reach a settled relationship that might regulate their future. Details of the failed Hussein-Arafat agreements in 1982-83 and the even more frustrating attempt at coordination in 1988 have this thread in common: the Palestinians will not grant Jordan senior partnership and Jordan will not grant the Palestinians a blank check of confederation. This difference had become clear even earlier when in 1974 Hussein made a major effort to redefine the Kingdom's constitution, apparently granting the West Bank (upon its return to Jordanian sovereignty) more weight. The "United Kingdom" scheme, however, failed to attract much support, undermining the King's claim to represent the Palestinians. Equally abortive was Amman's American-approved West Bank development plan, intended to hold off Palestinian immigration while reestablishing Jordanian influence. By 1988, when the King dramatically severed his remaining administrative and financial ties to the territories (greatly damaging both economies in the process), Hashemite influence among the Palestinians had sunk to a low ebb.

Now, as a consequence of the Gulf War, Jordan has been presented once more as an "option," albeit a rather passive one. Having gained Israeli assent by not doing the worst during the Gulf War, and American support for rejoining the winner's circle, the King has a further advantage as he enters negotiations—the Camp David Accords. Jordan can rely on the

Israelis to insist that the Self-Government be negotiated to resemble the Camp David autonomy framework which had Jordan "written in" at four points: 1) to serve as the delegation (in tandem with Palestinian participants "as agreed") negotiating the powers of the self-governing authority; 2) to negotiate with Israel on a "final status" and a Peace Treaty; 3) to participate in security arrangements, both externally with Israel and through a liaison with the "strong local police force"; and 4) to be part of the committee dealing with "the modalities of admission of persons displaced from the West Bank and Gaza in 1967" and other matters.

Thus King Hussein is highly advantaged without having to lift too many fingers. The Syrians, by attending a peace conference, allow him to go forward; the Palestinians, by joining his delegation, grant him legitimacy once more in Palestinian affairs. The King can let the Palestinians negotiate and compromise on the hard points while relying on Israel to insist that Jordan be given a key role in the workings of the Self-Government. (It bears noting, for example, that the lengthy Israeli-Jordanian experience in controlling border raids and terrorism will be an important asset in the security area.)

To sum up, Jordan can gain a practical role in the West Bank once more as part of an agreement that controls Palestinian nationalism but does not require the King to offend Palestinian sensibilities in the course of the negotiations. Palestinian Self-Government under these circumstances fits well what one long time observer of Hussein called his survival strategy: "no risks; no heroic initiatives. If possible—upset nobody: If a party must be upset, upset that which is least dangerous **now** . . . If there remains no way to survive but fight–fight brutally hard."[13]

A further advantage of the current diplomatic configuration is that Jordan's role can be rather passive. But while the King will certainly not put himself at odds with the Palestinians early on, there are two other considerations that may (or should) make him more active. First, an early failure of the negotiations, especially over symbolic issues such as Jerusalem, will set Jordan back when the country desperately needs calm and economic assistance to recover from the Gulf War's dislocations—including 250,000 new Palestinian

---

[13]Uriel Dann, *op. cit.*

refugees from the Gulf.[14] Second, the King's longer term interest lies in an agreement on final status that grants Jordan sovereignty either immediately or through a guaranteed fusion with a Palestinian entity. The worst outcome for the King would be a Self-Government that truly does turn into an independent Palestinian state—which then, from a position of relative strength, negotiates a confederation with Hashemite Jordan on its own terms or encourages a revolution against him. For reasons of his own dignity and a desire to show the Palestinians once and for all that their best choice lies with Jordan as senior partner, Hussein will want a speedy commencement of final status talks.

ISRAELI CHOICES

The Palestinians and the Jordanians may find themselves face-to-face with Self-Government by force of circumstance, but for Israel the matter is different. The Self-Government proposal was essentially invented by Israel. Now the issue is how far the Jewish state is prepared to go in defining it.

Yitzhak Shamir and his coalition are currently in a strong position. The Gulf War greatly diminished Israel's most dangerous short-term military threat—a combined Iraqi-Syrian attack on its eastern front—at very small cost to Israel itself. The Soviet Jewish immigrants are coming. And the Syrian interest in negotiation, for whatever reason, gives Shamir an opportunity to blunt the threat from Damascus. Simultaneously, Israel is only committed to negotiate Palestinian Self-Government in Judea, Samaria and the Gaza District but not to leave these territories.

These are the potential rewards of Israel's current situation. If they come to pass they will go far to consolidate a secure Jewish state in its historic homeland. Palestinian Self-Government is therefore a way to "square" the circle of indecision that has afflicted Israel ever since the tremendous victories of 1967.

---

[14]Jordan's officials describe the exodus as larger than that of 1967 and more harmful for the future—since no more remittances from the Gulf can be expected. See *Mideast Mirror,* August 14, 1991. See also Ann M. Lesch, "Palestinians in Kuwait," *Journal of Palestine Studies,* Volume XX, No .4, Summer 1991.

In a perfect world, most Israelis would prefer to have their state incorporate all the land west of the river. Few of any political persuasion believe that a return to the 1967 lines, even under peace, would be safe. Israelis are split on whether to trade "land for peace" or how much; but if they would do so, the King of Jordan is the preferred partner. A solid Israeli majority opposes a Palestinian state and the PLO is widely abhorred.

The *intifadah*, and then the Gulf War, had a paradoxical effect on those long-held Israeli positions. On one level, the personal level, the Israelis would rather be separate and distant from a Palestinian people many no longer trust in any capacity. But on another level, the majority stance against the establishment of a Palestinian (or even Jordanian) sovereignty any time soon in the territories was reinforced by Palestinian support for Saddam and by the mounting violence carried by Palestinians into pre-1967 Israel. And the Russian immigration has bolstered Israeli confidence that its demographic survival is well in hand and that it can dispense with the services of Palestinian laborers.

Likud's long held position that it would be unsafe (as well as morally and ideologically wrong) to give up the territories has thus been strengthened by recent events. But the drive to incorporate these territories was blunted long ago by fear that such a large influx of Arab citizens would turn Israel into a binational state. Today the idea of giving the Palestinians in the territories a choice of Israeli citizenship (a notion found in Begin's own autonomy proposal) has few takers, even in the Likud.

The conviction that Israel must control the territories but not absorb its inhabitants crosses party lines. Despite their long-standing differences over whether a territorial compromise might be acceptable, both Likud and Labour agree that in the absence of such a choice, Israel's objective is to hold on at minimal cost. While Shimon Peres as Prime Minister actively sought out a peace process, convinced that time was not entirely on Israel's side largely because of the corrupting consequences of ruling over a rebellious population, Yitzhak Shamir was content to wait, as Dayan once said of Egypt, for the telephone to ring.

It did ring for Dayan in 1973, when instead of bringing a call announcing Egypt's diplomatic capitulation it was the

Yom Kippur War on the other line; Shamir was similarly shaken in 1987 when the *intifadah* burst the illusion that the Palestinians were reconciled to a *status quo* moving steadily against them. The Unity Government was soon forced to solicit, shape and sometimes reject American diplomatic efforts to restart the peace process. But any search for ways to relieve Israel of responsibility for the Arab populations while not jeopardizing Israeli military control or right to settle could only lead to autonomy. Significantly, it was Rabin of the Labour Party who advocated a revival of autonomy even before Shamir.

Israel's interest in Palestinian Self-Government therefore goes deeper than the merely tactical or a desire to stall for time while the territories and their people are "absorbed." It does offer what Jabotinsky originally conceived: a way to deal with a "national minority" without destroying Israeli democracy or threatening the Jewish majority. And it fulfills the strictures of Moshe Dayan: to leave the Arabs alone as much as possible while sustaining a Jewish presence and military control in the area.

Israel's choice, however, is not just whether to advance the concept of Palestinian Self-Government but how to define its particulars. And it is here that the risks begin. These are both immediate and long term because they inevitably mean a loss of Israel's current control and imply a further loss as time goes on. The 1979-82 negotiations exposed these risks in three basic categories.

First, security dilemmas: It is possible for Israel to satisfy its external defense requirements in the territories (e.g. thwarting attack from Jordan or Syria) with an unobtrusive force. But even advances in technology will not eliminate the need for some defensive depth, which would entail demilitarization and control of certain areas. Much more problematical will be control of terrorism and the retention of Israeli intelligence assets. Security for external defense, the safety of settlers and the prevention of terrorism will require maximum cooperation with the Palestinians and the Jordanians—the "enemies" of the past.

Simultaneously, the Israelis will be looking to retain their capacity for unilateral action should such cooperation not be forthcoming. This is bound up with the otherwise legalistic-sounding argument over the "source" of authority for the actions of the Self-Government. If that source is not the Israeli military governor (even if his Administration is "withdrawn") but rather the Agreement itself or a Committee, then Israel will be spelling out rather intrusive procedures to control terrorism. This would be especially important when it comes to the settlements, because the settlers represent not only an ideological imperative for a Likud government but also a broader idea: that Jews should be safe wherever they live in the Land of Israel.

Second, political evolution: Once the Palestinians develop a functioning Self-Government, legitimized by elections and international support, it will be more difficult for Israel to resist the inevitable call for self-determination or at the least, a broadening set of powers that amount to Palestinian sovereignty. The transitional "Self-Government" negotiated by Israel would ironically become an Israeli Mandate for the emerging Arab state of Palestine. Aryeh Shalev, a former Israeli Military Governor of Judea and Samaria wrote in 1980 that, "the political will of the population under autonomy will have great influence on its future; and their desire is for an independent national entity."[15] The result he feared would be a state extracted from Israeli control under extreme local and international pressure.

Third, the political environment or "linkage": Israel faced this problem with Egypt and, as shown earlier, resisted any connection between her bilateral peace and the autonomy negotiations only to reverse course as the date for withdrawal from Sinai approached. Thus far, the Israelis have been content to suggest that the two tracks (Israel-Arab states; Israel-Palestinians) progress simultaneously but not that one cannot happen without the other. The interim nature of the Palestinian Self-Government, however, contrasts with the permanent nature of the peace treaties Israel will seek immediately with the other Arab states. If an agreement on Self-Government is reached, but the Israeli-Syrian negotiations fail, will the Syrians be able to veto it? And if the Israeli-Syrian negotiations succeed, but no agreement is reached on Self-

---

[15]See Aryeh Shalev, "Autonomy: Problems and Possible Solutions," *Jerusalem Quarterly* No. 15, Spring 1980, p. 14. Shalev also wrote a much larger study in Hebrew, published by Center for Strategic Studies of Tel Aviv University in 1979.

Government, will the Palestinians be able to veto the bilateral accords?

Overall, the danger for Israel can be expressed this way: Palestinian Self-Government could mean a loss of tangible control without much of a reduction in Palestinian (or Arab) hostility. At this point, Israel seems prepared to run that risk in the belief that improved relations with other Arab states and a "safe" Self-Government can be attained. The Israelis, like their negotiating counterparts, will be judging the details of the Self-Government against their longer-term objectives which still remain: presence in the territories, security guarantees and no independent Palestinian state.

In 1989, the then Unity Government was forced to consider where a renewed negotiation might take Israel—this time with the Palestinians. The resulting Shamir-Rabin plan reserved to Israel exclusive power in three areas: foreign policy, security and jurisdiction over Israeli citizens. Shamir's current coalition reaffirmed the "Peace Plan" when it took office. There is every reason to believe that these three points remain Israel's minimum—along with the exclusion of the city of Jerusalem from the jurisdiction of the Palestinian Self-Government.

VII LAND AND WATER, SECURITY AND PEACE

This analysis reveals many overlapping Palestinian, Jordanian and Israeli interests in Self-Government. The Palestinians may obtain what they cannot obtain otherwise: the end of military government, a way to halt Israeli encroachment and a chance to foster internationally-recognized, fairly-elected representatives. The Israelis can shed responsibility for the Palestinian population's security and prosperity, without losing their presence in the areas or jeopardizing their own security. The Jordanians can reenter the politics of the Palestinian problem on terms that give them an important and recognized role they do not now possess. Overall, then, Self-Government offers major advantages over the status quo.

The United States would be wise, however, to recognize that as in the earlier negotiations the parties are ultimately motivated by incompatible objectives. Though they will enter into negotiations by accepting that final status cannot be guaranteed in advance, once the process is in motion they will negotiate in the hopes of doing just that, through the struggle over the details of Self-Government. The Palestinians will pursue the symbols and powers of sovereignty, leading to a Palestinian state; the Jordanians, a confederal solution; Israel, either a prolongation of the interim arrangement or a three-way confederation. To achieve anything at all, American diplomats will have to act as a kind of conscience, emphasizing the interim nature of the negotiations and reminding the parties of the pragmatic advantages of changing the status quo.

There may even be rapid progress (as happened earlier) on elections (except for the role of East Jerusalem's Arabs), the size of the Self-Government and the list of minimal exclusive powers—the Israeli list of functions. But sooner or later, neither the appeal to conscience nor diplomatic ingenuity will avoid the hardest tests: the basic areas where agreement makes the entire Self-Government work and where disagreement makes even other achievements irrelevant.

At the end of 1980 and certainly by the spring of 1982, American negotiators had reduced the issues to five: 1) the source of authority; 2) ownership of land and water resources; 3) security; 4) settlements; and 5) Jerusalem. Of these, the "source of authority" problem will resolve itself if the parties can agree on everything else because in the end their agreement will be the real source of authority for Palestinian Self-Government. On the other side, Jerusalem is pre-eminently a final status issue. Its exclusion from the jurisdiction of Palestinian Self-Government, however, will not diminish the desire of the East Jerusalem Arabs themselves to cast their future with Palestinian, not Israeli, politics. Again, agreement on other matters will make a compromise solution more palatable if it enables the Palestinians to do this while the Israelis reaffirm their sovereignty. As experience attests, if Jerusalem becomes the first issue on the agenda, then hardly anything will happen.

The problems of the source of authority and Jerusalem will "break" a Self-Government negotiation only if the parties wish to do so. But agreement on those issues alone will not make a deal. For the real tests of Self-Government lie in two of the three remaining areas: control of land and water resources and security. And the third area—Jewish settlement activity—is really symbolic of both.

"Land-water" and "security" are really two sides of the same coin: the sense of safety for both Israelis and Palestinians. Safety consists of having (1) a "title," a right to be there and (2) physical safety, whether as individuals, as a community, or as a state.

The Israeli settlements are symptomatic of this basic problem. They constitute an Israeli title to the Land of Israel and, at least to some strategists, a guarantee that a threatening Palestinian "entity" can never be created. For the Palestinians, of course, the settlements show Israel's determination to remain whether wanted or not, a constant encroachment that threatens the Palestinian title. The Israelis are unlikely to trade anything on settlements outside of an overall agreement on Self-Government. And the Palestinians will never accept a Self-Government that does not give them some way to restrict settlements.

As noted, however, the settlements are really a "subset" of the issue of communal safety and control. Agreement on Self-Government (and the settlements problem) is therefore more likely to be found if the diplomats concentrate quickly on the key issues of "land-water" and "security." In each case, the U.S. can play a very important role in easing a way to solution. To repeat, if solutions are not found in these matters, the others will be insoluble as well.

LAND AND WATER

The land and water issue can be understood only in the context of the geographic and demographic realities now obtaining in the West Bank and Gaza.

Some 80 percent of the West Bank's 2,351 square miles is mountainous country, much of it barren; nearly half, the eastern part, is desert or semi-desert; and only 30 percent can be described as agricultural land. The yields of this land are low because the soil is stony and much of the farming is terraced on slopes. About 10 percent of the entire area (135,000 acres) is good farming country.

Water is scarce. The Jordan River's flow is already diminished by both Jordan and Israel, leaving little for the West Bank. Some 60 percent of the 432 Arab villages depend on rain water held in cisterns for household and other use. Little land is therefore irrigated. There are flows from part of the territory into the underground aquifers used by Israel's densely populated coastal plain. According to one source, these waters provide 17-19 percent of Israel's water supply and sustain the balance in the aquifer between fresh and saline sea water off the coast.[1]

---

[1] Report of JCSS Study Group, *The West Bank and Gaza: Israel's Options for Peace*, Tel Aviv, Tel Aviv University Press, 1989, p. 200. See also Meron Benvenisti and Shlomo Khayat, *The West Bank and Gaza Atlas*, Western Press, 1980, pp. 113-114, 118. And David Kahan, *Agriculture and Water*

The West Bank's farmland and water are thus severely limited, even if some way were found to use more of the water that otherwise flows to the coastal plain. As for other resources, the territory holds only large quantities of limestone rock and minerals from the Dead Sea, already being exploited by Israel from her coast within the "Green line," and by Jordan.

Population studies indicate that the Palestinian inhabitants number over 900,000, of whom 100,000 still live in refugee camps. The annual increase exceeds three percent and the historic outmigration (emigration) from the area to the Gulf and elsewhere has now largely ceased. People between the ages of 20-49 exceed 30 percent of the population. Half of all the inhabitants are urban; only 26 percent work in agriculture, versus 60 percent when the Israelis took over. And probably half the population depends—or depended, before the *intifadah*—largely on earnings from Israel.

Gaza, separated from the West Bank by a 26 mile portion of Israel's Negev desert, covers 151 square miles along the coast. It is a semi-arid plain with sufficient rain in the northern sector to support agriculture. About half the Gaza Strip is being cultivated with extensive irrigation: the crops are citrus and market gardens. The water supplies—drawing from the Israeli aquifer—are marginal at best, and becoming saline because of well overpumping. Gaza's Arab population, 354,000 according to the Israeli census of 1967, probably exceeds 660,000. Half the people still live in refugee camps and their birth rate is very high: 3.4 percent a year, much higher than the West Bank, while the emigration rate is much lower. Before the *intifadah*, 46 percent of the labor force worked in Israel. Doubtless, most of the employed Gazans draw (or drew) their income from Israel.[2]

Bearing upon these facts are Jewish and Arab immigration pressures. Up to a million Soviet Jews are expected in Israel over the next few years. Today, 80 percent of Israel's population

Resources of the West Bank and Gaza (1967-1987) (Boulder: Westview Press, 1987).

[2]The demographics and economics of the territories and their place in the peace process are discussed at length in Patrick Clawson and Howard Rosen, *The Economic Consequences of Peace for Israel, the Palestinians and Jordan,* (Washington D.C.: The Washington Institute for Near East Policy, 1991).

is Jewish (including Jerusalem). That proportion drops to 60 percent if the West Bank and Gaza are included. A 1988 study estimated that because of higher Arab birth rates (34.2 per thousand versus 13.1 per thousand for Jews) to keep the Jewish proportion of the whole at 60 percent by the year 2000, 700,000 Jewish immigrants would be needed over the next ten years.[3] Soviet immigration, then, goes a long way toward easing Israel's demographic worries, but does not end them.

The Palestinians, in addition to their refugees from the wars of 1948 and 1967, are in the midst of receiving another wave from the Gulf States. Some 250,000 have already arrived in Jordan. Both Jordan and various Palestinians have voiced the view that some population balance is a key to sustaining an Arab hold on the West Bank and Gaza. Thus "the right to return" to these areas will be of fundamental importance to a Palestinian Self-Government. The Palestinians already see this in relationship to Jewish settlements and the Israelis no doubt will hardly agree to such a return if Jewish settlements are to be menaced.

These facts indicate the following conclusions:

    1) the West Bank and Gaza contain a young, rapidly growing population;

    2) their land and water supplies are very limited and other natural resources are scant;

    3) the population is increasingly urban;

    4) its income depends largely on the Israeli economy, there being a very small agricultural base to begin with and very little industry or natural resources;

    5) the West Bank and Gaza have little in common, are physically separated and most importantly have very different ratios of settled population to refugees, Gaza containing many more people still living in camps.

A Palestinian Self-Government (Autonomy) for these areas would therefore need to foster large scale economic development if it were to attempt to improve the material condition of the population.

As an American participant in the earlier autonomy negotiations pointed out, "it would be difficult to imagine how

---

[3]JCSS study, *op. cit.*, p. 204.

the Palestinian self-governing authority could have meaningful responsibility in any field-industry, commerce, schools, agriculture, health—if it did not have authority over land, resources and water."[4] It is equally difficult, however, to see that authority vested exclusively in the Palestinians, not only because of Israeli objections but for purely practical reasons. A successful economic plan will require the (1) cooperation of Israel and Jordan and (2) additional foreign assistance, including regional arrangements on water.

The case for a shared and balanced power over land and water will clearly affect Jewish settlements. New and even expanded settlements will depend in large measure on the disposition of land, both public and private, and water resources, over which the Palestinian Self-Government must and will have a say.[5] A mutual veto over these resources as part of an overall agreement is more likely to bring a halt to new Israeli settlements than anything else.

---

[4]Alan J. Kreczko, "Support Reagan's Initiative," *Foreign Policy,* Winter 1982-83, p. 150.

[5]The land ownership system in the territories is far too complex to capture here. A number of factors including Ottoman era tax and conscription policies, illiteracy and fear, have left land-holding records incomplete or misleading. The British in their time established a register which remained during the Jordanian period. For the historical background, see Kenneth W. Stein, *The Land Question in Palestine, 1917-1939,* (Chapel Hill: University of North Carolina Press, 1984). After the Israeli Supreme Court invalidated an Israeli settlement, Eilon Moreh, built on private property confiscated for security reasons, an Israeli survey found that only half the land was "settled" legally, i.e. under legal title. The Israeli Military Government claims title to public lands (titled or untitled) and has an appeals process for those who have private claims. Clearly this land, plus land vacated by the withdrawal of Israeli military forces, would be logical patrimony of the Palestinian Self-Government. See Benvenisti and Khayat, *op. cit.*; also Plea Albeck, "The Use of State Owned Land in Judea and Samaria for Jewish Settlement," *Law and Legislation in Israel* No. 15, March 1984. See also William V. O'Brien *Law and Morality in Israel's War with the PLO,* (New York and London: Routledge, 1991), pp. 228-30 for Israel's not entirely coherent legal approach to the territories under military rule. For the Palestinian perspective, see "Urban Planning in the West Bank under Military Occupation," Summary Report, June 1991, by Anthony Coons for *Al-Haq,* the West Bank affiliate of the International Commission of Jurists. See also *The Rule of Law in the Areas Administered by Israel,* Israel Branch of the International Commission of Jurists, 1981.

Thus Israeli-Palestinian agreement on land and water should be set in a regional framework that includes not only Jordan but multilateral cooperation for both economic and political reasons. The United States is uniquely placed to facilitate the basic compromise by helping to make possible the external contribution that would enlarge the resources available to everyone.

SECURITY

"Security" broadly defined is the other serious test of whether Palestinian Self-Government can work. In the territories, security has three dimensions: defense against external attack, terrorism and crime. For both Israel and the Palestinians, communal and personal safety are at stake. The difficulties are compounded by differing definitions of terrorism and by the intelligence activities of the Israeli Military Administration, including paid informants.

As with land and water, the geopolitics of the territories play a major role in the security analysis. The map on page 94 shows how the terrain affects Israel's pre-1967 areas, including the strategic "down side" of the Samarian mountains as they slope toward Israel's narrow coastal plain. As noted earlier, the water resources of this area have also taken on a security dimension.[6]

The real issue of external defense, however, is the role of the territories in Israel's overall military strategy. Two aspects drawn from the history of the Arab-Israeli conflict are paramount: first, the territories might be used to launch an armored attack intended to split pre-1967 Israel in two at its narrowest point; second, Israeli mobilization on the coastal plain could be disrupted by artillery or rocket attack from the West Bank. Against this, various Israeli military analysts have

---

[6]Some Israeli analysts believe Israel should insist on annexing a narrow strip in the Samarian foothills, in some places no more than six or seven meters, that would cover the main drains into the aquifer so as to "limit the possibility of acute friction over water resources." See Ze'ev Schiff, *Security for Peace: Israel's Minimum Security Requirements in Negotiations with the Palestinians,* (Washington D.C.: The Washington Institute for Near East Policy, Policy Paper No. 15, 1989), p. 24. Also Saul B. Cohen, *The Geopolitics of Israel's Border Question,* (Boulder: Westview, 1986).

CENTRAL AND NORTHERN ISRAEL AND OCCUPIED TERRITORIES

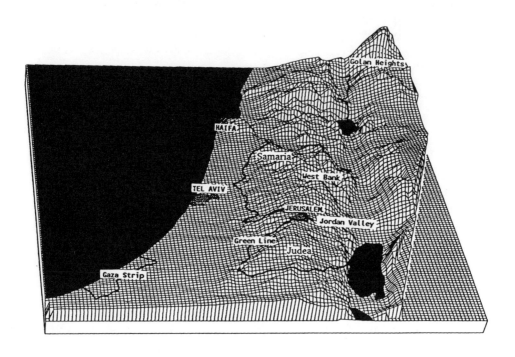

Significant Distances between Localities:

Green Line—Tel Aviv...............................23 kilometers
Jordan River—Tel Aviv...........................70 kilometers
Gaza—Green Line.....................................42 kilometers
Jerusalem—Jordan River.........................31 kilometers

concluded that "full demilitarization, Israeli warning stations in the area and Israeli control of some of the areas, such as the Jordan Valley and Ma'ale Adumim" would be sufficient.[7] And it can be argued that holding on to the Arab population centers could actually weaken Israel in time of conflict because scarce forces would have to be committed to restrain a hostile population.

Following the Gulf War, a reappraisal of Israel's deterrent strategy is underway and the early returns are predictably mixed. Clearly, Israel's mobilization areas can be disrupted by long-range missile fire even if Israel retains the territories. Just as clearly, territory does play a role in giving the defender time and depth in a war where technology far extends the battlefield.[8]

It is possible to imagine various and quite elaborate arrangements that would minimize Israel's security presence while maximizing her early warning capabilities. These include satellite capabilities Israel cannot now afford; warning sensors; troop developments along the Eastern slopes of the West Bank and the Jordan Valley (where few Palestinians live); electronic warning stations; anti-aircraft missiles; and anti-missile missiles.[9] An exclusive Israeli control over external security is therefore quite feasible without a continuing massive intrusion on the Palestinians. But the essential point in external defense is always the external threat. And for Israel that means the power of the so-called Arab Eastern Front—potentially Syria, Jordan, Iraq and Saudi Arabia.

The defeat of Iraq in the Gulf War, as even the Syrians admit, dramatically weakened what had become a semi-cooperative Eastern Front against Israel. Before the war, Jordan in particular, while careful not to violate Israeli "red-lines" by allowing Iraqi forces into Jordan itself, had developed important intelligence and other exchanges with the Iraqis. A

---

[7]See for example, former Chief of Staff Mordechai Gur in *Ha'aretz*, June 12-13, 1988.

[8]Ze'ev Schiff, "Israel after the War," *Foreign Affairs*, Spring 1991, pp. 19-33.

[9]See Schiff, *op. cit.*, pp. 55-57.

coordinated air defense system was also implicit in the deployments of Jordanian, Iraqi and Syrian capabilities.

While the Eastern Front is a far less ominous threat for now, the Israelis will continue to plan for that possibility.[10] Much depends not only on the course of Syrian arms acquistions, but also on the recovery of Iraq. In any event, for the West Bank to become a battleground would constitute a disaster for both Israel and the Palestinians.

From the foregoing a singular conclusion can be drawn. Israel's minimal security requirements in the West Bank for external defense will be heavily influenced by the potential threat of the Eastern Front. Or to put it another way, the participation of Jordan in the security arrangements for the territories and the state of Israeli-Syrian relations will have a major influence on Israeli security flexibility.

The American role in these security arrangements can be quite significant. Three elements are likely to be crucial. One will concern U.S.-Israel intelligence exchanges, such as access to satellite surveillance; a second will be a monitoring function. The third, however, will be more important than all the rest. That is the American role as the "partner" not only to the Self-Government agreement but to the other track—the overall strategic relationship between Israel and the other Arab states. A Palestinian Self-Government functioning in the shadow of Syrian or Gulf Arab hostility will have a much rougher go than one functioning in the context of peaceful relations—even a cold peace—between the Arab states and Israel.

The other critical aspects of security are internal. Public order—the policeman on the beat—will assuredly be a main responsibility of the Palestinian Self-Government. Just as assuredly, at least at the start, it will have to rely on Jordanian (and Israeli) cooperation to work. The more difficult issue concerns not street crime but terrorism.

It is hard to avoid the conclusion that no outside party can substitute for a measure of trust in this area among Israel, Jordan and the Palestinian Self-Government. This is a very circular argument, it being clear already that if such trust were possible much of the heat would have already gone out of the entire conflict. Moreover, the Palestinians themselves have been badly hurt by internecine warfare. More than one-third

---

[10] *Ibid.* The Syrians still mount a powerful force on their own.

of those slain during the *intifadah* have been victims of fellow Arabs. Even at full strength, the Israeli Military Government has not been able to impose absolute order or to assure total safety for those suspected rightly or wrongly of being informants. The continued presence of Israeli settlers will not make the task of public order any easier.

Terrorism is therefore likely to continue despite everyone's best efforts, even under Palestinian Self-Government. The issue is whether such terrorism, defined as attacks on civilians, will find in the Self-Government a source of support, refuge and immunity. "Trust" in this case will be the confidence of the parties that the Self-Government will act to suppress terrorism and that the Israelis will not use it as an excuse to run roughshod over Palestinian authority. Above all, terrorism will have to be viewed by most of the Palestinian population as a real threat to their interests.

In the establishment of such trust, tacit "red-lines" among the parties will have to be created and understood, and the United States will be called upon sooner or later to "vouch" for these lines. In the event of a crisis, Washington's impartial judgement will count heavily as to whether the parties involved upheld their commitments. A Palestinian Self-Government that cannot prevent its opponents from acting to harm its own interests will fail. Israel should have every interest in making sure that the Self-Government succeed without Israeli intervention, as should Jordan. But no one can expect "self-policing" to work perfectly at the outset of what will be a controversial agreement. This is where U.S. support and good offices will be most useful.

CONCLUSION: THE COUNSEL OF IMPERFECTION

Churchill once said that "the maxim—nothing avails but perfection—spells paralysis." The American policymaker in search of the perfect solution to the Palestinian problem—or the Arab-Israeli conflict—will find only paralysis. The parties are faced instead with the choice of doing better than the status quo or hoping that something better will turn up to relieve them of the necessity for compromise.

Palestinian Self-Government (Autonomy) is a counsel of imperfection. By nature, imperfections limit, yet within those limits much can be achieved. Given the ferocious antagonisms of the Arab-Israeli conflict, perhaps the first argument in favor of Palestinian "Self-Government is the negative: what it prevents.

In the Arab-Israeli conflict there are no truly new ideas, only good ones and bad ones—depending on one's point of view. Palestinian Self-Government as an interim solution can be seen as a good idea if each side sees it as a necessary obstacle to the other's aspirations. The Palestinians' only hope is to convert Self-Government into the strategic ally they lack. If the Palestinians see it as the best way available to prevent Israeli annexation they will swallow the inevitable limitations it entails. If Israelis see it as the best way available to prevent a Palestinian state—or at least the economic and human disaster that would revive demands for such a state—then they will run the risks of fostering limited political institutions in the territories.

There is also a strong positive argument for Self-Government, in that it can give each party what it does not now possess: for the Palestinians, the end of Israeli Military Government, some control over resources, democratic political institutions, and some help for refugees; for Jordan, a recognized role in West Bank affairs, especially with regard to security; for Israel, less responsibility for the Palestinian population, limited loss of security and a confirmed civilian presence; and for all of the parties, a contraction in hostility and an expansion of hope.

The United States can help all of this come about. American policy can remind the parties that differences on final status can impede interim steps. Washington can work to assure a supporting cast: productive Israel-Arab state negotiations to contain those who reject the peacemakers; regional arrangements to enlarge water resources and economic exchange; and security agreements that monitor performance and encourage trust. This seems a great deal of effort for what is billed as an interim agreement. Yet as the alternative to paralysis it offers critical steps down the path at the end of which a lasting solution may be found. Palestinian Self-Government can contribute to the establishment of peace. If the parties are not convinced of this, then Self-Government will continue to be the road not taken. If the parties are convinced, then it will happen and very soon.

APPENDICES

APPENDIX I
SECURITY COUNCIL RESOLUTION 242
CONCERNING PRINCIPLES FOR A JUST AND
LASTING PEACE IN THE MIDDLE EAST
November 22, 1967

The Security Council,

Expressing its continuing concern with the grave situation in the Middle East,

Emphasizing the inadmissibility of the acquisition of territory by war and the need to work for a just and lasting peace in which every State in the area can live in security,

Emphasizing further that all Member States in their acceptance of the Charter of the United Nations have undertaken a commitment to act in accordance with Article 2 of the Charter,

1. *Affirms* that the fulfillment of Charter principles requires the establishment of a just and lasting peace in the Middle East which should include the application of both the following principles:
(i) Withdrawal of Israeli armed forces from territories occupied in the recent conflict;
(ii) Termination of all claims or states of belligerency and respect for and acknowledgement of the sovereignty, territorial integrity and political independence of every State in the area and their right to live in peace within secure and recognized boundaries free from threats or acts of force;

2. *Affirms further* the necessity
(a) For guaranteeing freedom of navigation through international waterways in the area;
(b) For achieving a just settlement of the refugee problem;
(c) For guaranteeing the territorial inviolability and political independence of every State in the area, through measures including the establishment of demilitarized zones;

3. *Requests* the Secretary-General to designate a Special Representative to proceed to the Middle East to establish and maintain contacts with the States concerned in order to promote agreement and assist efforts to achieve a peaceful and accepted settlement in accordance with the provisions and principles in this resolution;

4. *Requests* the Secretary-General to report to the Security Council of the progress of the efforts of the Special Representative as soon as possible.

APPENDIX II
SECURITY COUNCIL RESOLUTION 338
CONCERNING THE OCTOBER WAR
October 22, 1973

The Security Council,

1. *Calls upon* all parties to the present fighting to cease all firing and terminate all military activity immediately, no later than 12 hours after the moment of the adoption of this decision, in the positions they now occupy;

2. *Calls upon* the parties concerned to start immediately after the cease-fire the implementation of Security Council 242 (1967) in all of its parts;

3. *Decides* that, immediately and concurrently with the cease-fire, negotiations start between the parties concerned under appropriate auspices aimed at establishing a just and durable peace in the Middle East.

APPENDIX III
THE PEACE PLAN OF ISRAEL AS PRESENTED IN A SPEECH OF PRIME MINISTER MENACHEM BEGIN IN THE KNESSET[1]
December 28, 1977

Mr. Chairman, respected Knesset members, with the establishment of peace, we shall propose to introduce administrative autonomy for the Arab residents of Judea, Samaria and the Gaza District on the basis of the following principles:

1. The administration of the military government in Judea, Samaria and the Gaza District will be abolished.

2. In Judea, Samaria and the Gaza District, administrative autonomy of the Arab residents, by and for them, will be established.

---

[1]Source: Aryeh Shalev, *The Autonomy—Problems and Possible Solutions,* Paper No. 8, Jan. 1980, Center for Strategic Studies, Tel Aviv University. The translation was taken from: British Broadcast Corporation (B.B.C.), Survey of World broadcasting (SWB), Middle East and North Africa, ME/5702/A/1, 30.12.77; and from *Near East Report,* Volume XXII, No. 29, July 19, 1978.

3. The residents of Judea, Samaria and the Gaza District will elect an administrative council composed of 11 members. The administrative council will operate in accordance with the principles laid down in this paper.

4. Any resident, 18 years old and above, without distinction of citizenship, or if stateless, is entitled to vote in the elections to the administrative council.

5. Any resident whose name is included in the list of candidates for the administrative council and who, on the day the list is submitted, is 25 years old or above, is entitled to be elected to the council.

6. The administrative council will be elected by general, direct, personal, equal and secret ballot.

7. The period of office of the administrative council will be four years from the day of its election.

8. The administrative council will sit in Bethlehem.

9. All the administrative affairs relating to the Arab residents of the area of Judea, Samaria and the Gaza District, will be under the direction and within the competence of the administrative council.

10. The administrative council will operate the following departments: education, religious affairs, finance, transportation, construction and housing, industry, commerce and tourism, agriculture, health, labor and social welfare, rehabilitation of refugees, and the department for the administration of justice and the supervision of the local police force, and promulgate regulations relating to the operations of these departments.

11. Security and public order in the areas of Judea, Samaria and the Gaza District will be the responsibility of the Israeli authorities.

12. The administrative council will elect its own chairman.

13. The first session of the administrative council will be convened 30 days after the publication of the election results.

14. Residents of Judea, Samaria and the Gaza District, without distinction of citizenship, or if stateless, will be granted free choice (option) of either Israeli or Jordanian citizenship.

15. A resident of the areas of Judea, Samaria and the Gaza District who requests Israeli citizenship will be granted such citizenship in accordance with the citizenship law of the state.

16. Residents of Judea, Samaria and the Gaza District who are citizens of Jordan or who, in accordance with the right of free option, choose Israeli citizenship, will be entitled to vote for, and be elected to the Knesset in accordance with the election law.

17. Residents of Judea, Samaria, and the Gaza District who are citizens of Jordan or who, in accordance with the right of free option will become citizens of Jordan, will elect and be eligible for election to the parliament of the Hashemite Kingdom of Jordan in accordance with the election law of that country.

18. Questions arising from the vote to the Jordanian parliament by residents of Judea, Samaria and the Gaza District will be clarified in negotiations between Israel and Jordan.

19. A committee will be established of representatives of Israel, Jordan and the administrative council to examine existing legislation in Judea, Samaria and the Gaza District and to determine which legislation will continue in force, which will be abolished and what will be the competence of the administrative council to promulgate regulations. The rulings of the committee will be adopted by unanimous decisions.

20. Residents of Israel will be entitled to acquire land and settle in the areas of Judea, Samaria and the Gaza Districts. Arabs, residents of Judea, Samaria and the Gaza District who, in accordance with the free options granted them, will become Israeli citizens, will be entitled to acquire land and settle in Israel.

21. A committee will be established of representatives of Israel, Jordan and the administrative council to determine norms of immigration to the areas of Judea, Samaria and the Gaza District. The committee will determine the norms whereby Arab refugees residing outside Judea, Samaria and the Gaza District will be permitted to immigrate to these areas in reasonable numbers. The ruling of the committee will be adopted by unanimous decision.

22. Residents of Israel and residents of Judea, Samaria and the Gaza District will be assured of movement and freedom of economic activity in Israel, Judea, Samaria and the Gaza District.

23. The administrative council will appoint one of its members to represent the council before the Government of Jordan for deliberation on matters of common interest.

24. Israel stands by its right and its claim of sovereignty to Judea, Samaria and the Gaza District. In the knowledge that other claims exist, it proposes for the sake of the agreement and the peace, that the question of sovereignty be left open.

25. With regard to the administration of the holy places of the three religions in Jerusalem, a special proposal will be drawn up and submitted that will include the guarantee of freedom of access to members of all faiths to the shrines holy to them.

26. These principles will be subject to review after a five-year period.

Mr. Chairman, I must now explain the 11th clause of this plan, as well as the 24th clause.

Esteemed Knesset members: In the 11th clause of our plan we postulated: The security and public order of the areas of Judea, Samaria and the Gaza District will be entrusted to the hands of the Israeli authorities. Without this clause there is no meaning to the plan of administrative autonomy. I wish to announce from the Knesset rostrum that this self-evidently includes deployment of IDF forces in Judea, Samaria and in the Gaza Strip.

APPENDIX IV
THE CAMP DAVID ACCORDS
September 17, 1978

A FRAMEWORK FOR PEACE IN THE MIDDLE EAST AGREED AT CAMP DAVID

Mohammed Anwar al-Sadat, President of the Arab Republic of Egypt, and Menachem Begin, Prime Minister of Israel, met with Jimmy Carter, President of the United States of America, at Camp David from September 5 to September 17, 1978, and have agreed on the following framework for peace in the Middle East. They invite other parties to the Arab-Israeli conflict to adhere to it.

PREAMBLE

The search for peace in the Middle East must be guided by the following:

—The agreed basis for a peaceful settlement of the conflict between Israel and its neighbors is United Nations Security Council Resolution 242, in all its parts.

—After four wars during thirty years, despite intensive human efforts, the Middle East, which is the cradle of civilization and the birthplace of three great religions, does not yet enjoy the blessings of peace. The people of the Middle East yearn for peace so that the vast human and natural resources of the region can be turned to the pursuits of peace and so that this area can become a model for coexistence and cooperation among nations.

—The historic initiative of President Sadat in visiting Jerusalem and the reception accorded to him by the Parliament, government and people of Israel, and the reciprocal visit of Prime Minister Begin to Ismailia, the peace proposals made by both leaders, as well as the warm reception of these missions by the peoples of both countries, have created an unprecedented opportunity for peace which must not be lost if this generation and future generations are to be spared the tragedies of war.

—The provisions of the Charter of the United Nations and the other accepted norms of international law and legitimacy now provide accepted standards for the conduct of relations among all states.

—To achieve a relationship of peace, in the spirit of Article 2 of the United Nations Charter, future negotiations between Israel and any neighbor prepared to negotiate peace and security with it, are necessary for the purpose of carrying out all the provisions and principles of Resolutions 242 and 338.

—Peace requires respect for the sovereignty, territorial integrity and political independence of every state in the area and their right to live in peace within secure and recognized boundaries free from threats or acts of force. Progress toward that goal can accelerate movement toward a new era of reconciliation in the Middle East marked by cooperation in promoting economic development, in maintaining stability, and in assuring security.

—Security is enhanced by a relationship of peace and by cooperation between nations which enjoy normal relations. In addition, under the terms of peace treaties, the parties can, on the basis of reciprocity, agree to special security arrangements such as demilitarized zones, limited armaments areas, early warning stations, the presence of international forces, liaison, agreed measures for monitoring, and other arrangements that they agree are useful.

FRAMEWORK

Taking these factors into account, the parties are determined to reach a just, comprehensive, and durable settlement of the Middle East conflict through the conclusion of peace treaties based on Security Council Resolutions 242 and 338 in all their parts. Their purpose is to achieve peace and good neighborly relations. They recognize that, for peace to endure, it must involve all those who have been most deeply affected by the conflict. They therefore agree that this framework as appropriate is intended by them to constitute a basis for peace not only between Egypt and Israel, but also between Israel and each of its other neighbors which is prepared to negotiate peace with Israel on this basis. With that objective in mind, they have agreed to proceed as follows:

A. West Bank and Gaza

1. Egypt, Israel, Jordan and the representatives of the Palestinian people should participate in negotiations on the resolution of the Palestinian problem in all its aspects. To achieve that objective, negotiations relating to the West Bank and Gaza should proceed in three stages:

(a)   Egypt and Israel agree that, in order to ensure a peaceful and orderly transfer of authority, and taking into account the security concerns of all the parties, there should be transitional arrangements for the West Bank and Gaza for a period not exceeding five years. In order to provide full autonomy to the inhabitants, under these arrangements the Israeli military government and its civilian administration will be withdrawn as soon as a self-governing authority has been freely elected by the inhabitants of these areas to replace the existing military government. To negotiate the details of a transitional arrangement, the Government of Jordan will be invited to join the negotiations on the basis of this framework. These new arrangements should give due consideration both to the principle of self-government by the inhabitants of these territories and to the legitimate security concerns of the parties involved.

(b)   Egypt, Israel, and Jordan will agree on the modalities for establishing the elected self-governing authority in the West Bank and Gaza. The delegations of Egypt and Jordan may include Palestinians from the West Bank and Gaza or other Palestinians as mutually agreed. The parties will negotiate an agreement which will define the powers and responsibilities of the self-governing authority to be exercised in the West Bank and Gaza. A withdrawal of Israeli armed forces will take place and there will be a redeployment of the remaining Israeli forces into specified security locations. The agreement will also include arrangements for assuring internal and external security and public order. A strong local police force will be established, which may include Jordanian citizens. In addition, Israeli and Jordanian forces will participate in joint patrols and in the manning of control posts to assure the security of the borders.

(c)   When the self-governing authority (administrative council) in the West Bank and Gaza is established and inaugurated, the transitional period of five years will begin. As soon as possible, but not later than the third year after the beginning of the transitional period, negotiations will take place to determine the final status of the West Bank and Gaza and its relationship with its neighbors, and to conclude a peace treaty between Israel and Jordan by the end of the transitional period. These negotiations will be conducted among Egypt, Israel, Jordan, and the elected representatives of the inhabitants of the West Bank and Gaza. Two separate but related committees will be convened, one committee, consisting of representatives of the four parties which will negotiate and agree on the final status of the West Bank and Gaza, and its relationship with its neighbors, and the second committee, consisting of representatives of Israel and representatives of Jordan to be joined by the elected representatives of the inhabitants of the West Bank and Gaza, to negotiate the peace treaty between Israel and Jordan, taking into account the agreement reached on the final status of the West Bank and Gaza. The negotiations shall be based on all the provisions and principles of UN Security Council Resolution 242. The negotiations will resolve, among other matters, the location of the boundaries and the nature of the security arrangements.

The solution from the negotiations must also recognize the legitimate rights of the Palestinian people and their just requirements. In this way, the Palestinians will participate in the determination of their own future through:

(1) The negotiations among Egypt, Israel, Jordan and the representatives of the inhabitants of the West Bank and Gaza to agree on the final status of the West Bank and Gaza and other outstanding issues by the end of the transitional period.

(2) Submitting their agreement to a vote by the elected representatives of the inhabitants of the West Bank and Gaza.

(3) Providing for the elected representatives of the inhabitants of the West Bank and Gaza to decide how they shall govern themselves consistent with the provisions of their agreement.

(4) Participating as stated above in the work of the committee negotiating the peace treaty between Israel and Jordan.

2. All necessary measures will be taken and provisions made to assure the security of Israel and its neighbors during the transitional period and beyond. To assist in providing such security, a strong local police force will be constituted by the self-governing authority. It will be composed of inhabitants of the West Bank and Gaza. The police will maintain continuing liaison on internal security matters with the designated Israeli, Jordanian and Egyptian officers.

3. During the transitional period, representatives of Egypt, Israel, Jordan, and the self-governing authority will constitute a continuing committee to decide by agreement on the modalities of admission of persons displaced from the West Bank and Gaza in 1967, together with necessary measures to prevent disruption and disorder. Other matters of common concern may also be dealt with by this committee.

4. Egypt and Israel will work with each other and with other interested parties to establish agreed procedures for a prompt, just and permanent implementation of the resolution of the refugee problem.

B. Egypt-Israel

1. Egypt and Israel undertake not to resort to the threat or the use of force to settle disputes. Any disputes shall be settled by peaceful means in accordance with the provisions of Article 33 of the Charter of the United Nations.

2. In order to achieve peace between them, the parties agree to negotiate in good faith with a goal of concluding within three months from the signing of the Framework a peace treaty between them while inviting the other parties to the conflict to proceed simultaneously to negotiate and conclude similar peace treaties with a view to achieving a comprehensive peace in the area. The Framework for the Conclusion of a Peace Treaty between Egypt and Israel will govern the peace negotiations between them. The parties will agree on the modalities and the timetable for the implementation of their obligations under the treaty.

C. Associated Principles

1. Egypt and Israel state that the principles and provisions described below should apply to peace treaties between Israel and each of its neighbors—Egypt, Jordan, Syria and Lebanon.

2. Signatories shall establish among themselves relationships normal to states at peace with one another. To this end, they should undertake to abide by all the provisions of the charter of the United Nations. Steps to be taken in this respect include:
   (a) full recognition;
   (b) abolishing economic boycotts;
   (c) guaranteeing that under their jurisdiction the citizens of the other parties shall enjoy the protection of the due process of law.

3. Signatories should explore possibilities for economic development in the context of final peace treaties, with the objective of contributing to the atmosphere of peace, cooperation and friendship which is their common goal.

4. Claims Commissions may be established for the mutual settlement of all financial claims.

5. The United States shall be invited to participate in the talks on matters related to the modalities of the implementation of the agreements and working out the timetable for the carrying out of the obligation of the parties.

6. The United Nations Security Council shall be requested to endorse the peace treaties and ensure that their provisions shall not be violated. The permanent members of the Security Council shall be requested to underwrite the peace treaties and ensure respect for their provisions.

They shall also be requested to conform their policies and actions with the undertakings contained in this Framework.

For the Government of the Arab Republic of Egypt: *A. Sadat*

For the Government of the Israel: *M. Begin*

Witnessed by: *Jimmy Carter*
Jimmy Carter, President of
the United States of America

FRAMEWORK FOR THE CONCLUSION OF A PEACE TREATY BETWEEN EGYPT AND ISRAEL

In order to achieve peace between them, Israel and Egypt agree to negotiate in good faith with a goal of concluding within three months of the signing of this framework a peace treaty between them.

It is agreed that:

The site of the negotiations will be under a United Nations flag at a location or locations to be mutually agreed.

All of the principles of UN Resolution 242 will apply in this resolution of the dispute between Israel and Egypt.

Unless otherwise mutually agreed, terms of the peace treaty will be implemented between two and three years after the peace treaty is signed.

The following matters are agreed between the parties:

(a) the full exercise of Egyptian sovereignty up to the internationally recognized border between Egypt and mandated Palestine;

(b) the withdrawal of Israeli armed forces from the Sinai;

(c) the use of airfields left by the Israelis near El Arish, Rafah, Ras en Naqb, and Sharm el Sheikh for civilian purposes only, including possible commercial use by all nations;

(d) the right of free passage by ships of Israel through the Gulf of Suez and the Suez Canal on the basis of the Constantinople Convention of 1888 applying to all nations; the Strait of Tiran and the Gulf of Aqaba are international waterways to be open to all nations for unimpeded and nonsuspendable freedom of navigation and overflight;

(e) the construction of a highway between the Sinai and Jordan near Eilat with guaranteed free and peaceful passage by Egypt and Jordan; and

(f) the stationing of military forces listed below.

STATIONING OF FORCES

A. No more than one division (mechanized or infantry) of Egyptian armed forces will be stationed within an area lying approximately 50 kilometers (km) east of the Gulf of Suez and the Suez Canal.

B. Only United Nations forces and civil police equipped with light weapons to perform normal police functions will be stationed within an area lying west of the international border and the Gulf of Aqaba, varying in width from 20 km to 40 km.

C. In the area within 3 km east of the international border there will be Israeli limited military forces not to exceed four infantry battalions and United Nations observers.

D. Border patrol units, not to exceed three battalions, will supplement the civil police in maintaining order in the area not included above.

The exact demarcation of the above areas will be as decided during the peace negotiations.

Early warning stations may exist to insure compliance with the terms of the agreement.

United Nations forces will be stationed: (a) in part of the area in the Sinai lying within about 20 km of the Mediterranean Sea and adjacent to the international border, and (b) in the Sharm el Sheikh are to ensure freedom of passage through the Straits of Tiran; and these forces will not be removed unless such removal is approved by the Security Council of the United Nations with a unanimous vote of the five permanent members.

After a peace treaty is signed, and after the interim withdrawal is complete, normal relations will be established between Egypt and Israel, including: full recognition, including diplomatic, economic and cultural relations; termination of economic boycotts and barriers to the free movement of goods and people; and mutual protection of citizens by the due process of law.

INTERIM WITHDRAWAL

Between three months and nine months after the signing of the peace treaty, all Israeli forces will withdraw east of a line extending from a point east of El Arish to Ras Muhammad, the exact location of this line to be determined by mutual agreement.

For the Government of the Arab Republic of Egypt: *A. Sadat*

For the Government of Israel: *M. Begin*

Witnessed by: *Jimmy Carter*
Jimmy Carter, President of
the United States of America

LETTER FROM EGYPTIAN PRESIDENT ANWAR AL-SADAT TO PRESIDENT JIMMY CARTER
September 17, 1978

Dear Mr. President:

I am writing you to reaffirm the position of the Arab Republic of Egypt with respect to Jerusalem:

1. Arab Jerusalem is an integral part of the West Bank. Legal and historical Arab rights in the City must be respected and restored.

2. Arab Jerusalem should be under Arab sovereignty.

3. The Palestinian inhabitants of Arab Jerusalem are entitled to exercise their legitimate national rights, being part of the Palestinian People in the West Bank.

4. Relevant Security Council Resolutions, particularly Resolutions 242 and 267, must be applied with regard to Jerusalem. All the measures taken by Israel to alter the status of the City are null and void and should be rescinded.

5. All peoples must have free access to the City and enjoy the free exercise of worship and the right to visit and transit to the holy places without distinction or discrimination.

6. The holy places of each faith may be placed under the administration and control of their representatives.

7. Essential functions in the City should be undivided and a joint municipal council composed of an equal number of Arab and Israeli members can supervise the carrying out of these functions. In this way, the City shall be undivided.

Sincerely,

Mohammed Anwar al-Sadat

LETTER FROM ISRAELI PRIME MINISTER MENACHEM BEGIN TO PRESIDENT JIMMY CARTER
September 17, 1978

Dear Mr. President:

I have the honor to inform you, Mr. President, that on June 28, 1967—Israel's Parliament (The Knesset) promulgated and adopted a law to the effect: "the Government is empowered by a decree to apply the law, the jurisdiction and administration of the State to any part of Eretz Israel (land of Israel-Palestine), as stated in that decree."

On the basis of this law, the Government of Israel decreed in July 1967 that Jerusalem is one city indivisible, the Capital of the State of Israel.

Sincerely,

Menachem Begin

LETTER FROM EGYPTIAN PRESIDENT ANWAR AL-SADAT TO PRESIDENT JIMMY CARTER
September 17, 1978

Dear Mr. President:

In connection with the "Framework for Peace in the Middle East," I am writing you this letter to inform you of the position of the Arab Republic of Egypt, with respect to the implementation of the comprehensive settlement.

To ensure the implementation of the provisions related to the West Bank and Gaza and in order to safeguard the legitimate rights of the Palestinian people, Egypt will be prepared to assume the Arab role emanating from these provisions, following consultations with Jordan and the representatives of the Palestinian people.

Sincerely,

Mohammed Anwar al-Sadat

LETTER FROM PRESIDENT JIMMY CARTER TO EGYPTIAN PRESIDENT ANWAR AL-SADAT
September 22, 1978

Dear Mr. President:

I have received your letter of September 17, 1978, setting forth the Egyptian position on Jerusalem. I am transmitting a copy of that letter to Prime Minister Begin for his information.

The position of the United States on Jerusalem remains as stated by Ambassador Goldberg in the United Nations General Assembly on July 14, 1967, and subsequently by Ambassador Yost in the United Nations Security Council on July 1, 1969.

Sincerely,

Jimmy Carter

LETTER FROM PRESIDENT JIMMY CARTER TO ISRAELI PRIME MINISTER MENACHEM BEGIN
September 22, 1978

Dear Mr. Prime Minister:

I hereby acknowledge that you have informed me as follows:

A) In each paragraph of the Agreed Framework Document the expressions "Palestinians" or "Palestinian People" are being and will be construed and understood by you as "Palestinian Arabs."

B) In each paragraph in which the expression "West Bank" appears, it is being, and will be, understood by the Government of Israel as Judea and Samaria.

Sincerely,

Jimmy Carter

APPENDIX V
LETTER FROM ISRAELI PRIME MINISTER MENACHEM BEGIN
AND EGYPTIAN PRESIDENT ANWAR AL-SADAT
TO PRESIDENT JIMMY CARTER
March 26, 1979

Dear Mr. President:

This letter confirms that Egypt and Israel have agreed as follows:

The Governments of Egypt and Israel recall that they concluded at Camp David and signed at the White House on September 17, 1978, the annexed documents entitled "A Framework for Peace in the Middle East Agreed at Camp David" and "Framework for the Conclusion of a Peace Treaty between Egypt and Israel."

For the purpose of achieving a comprehensive peace settlement in accordance with the above-mentioned Frameworks, Egypt and Israel will proceed with the implementation of those provisions relating to the West Bank and the Gaza Strip. They have agreed to start negotiations within a month after the exchange of the instruments of ratification of the Peace Treaty. In accordance with the "Framework for Peace in the Middle East," the Hashemite Kingdom of Jordan is invited to join the negotiations. The Delegation of Egypt and Jordan may include Palestinians from the West Bank and Gaza Strip or other Palestinians as mutually agreed. The purpose of the negotiation shall be to agree, prior to the elections, on the modalities for establishing the elected self-governing authority (administrative council), define its powers and responsibilities, and agree upon other related issues. In the event Jordan decides not to take part in the negotiations, the negotiations will be held by Egypt and Israel.

The two Governments agree to negotiate continuously and in good faith to conclude these negotiations at the earliest possible date. They also agree that the objective of the negotiations is the establishment of the self-governing authority in the West Bank and Gaza in order to provide full autonomy to the inhabitants.

Egypt and Israel set for themselves the goal of completing the negotiations within one year so that elections will be held as expeditiously as possible after agreement has been reached between the parties. The self-governing authority referred to in the "Framework for Peace in the Middle East" will be established and inaugurated within one month after it has been elected, at which time the transitional period of five years will begin. The Israeli military government and its civilian administration will be withdrawn, to be replaced by the self-governing authority, as specified in the "Framework for Peace in the Middle East." A withdrawal of Israeli armed forces will then take place and there will be a redeployment of the remaining Israeli forces into specified security locations.

This letter also confirms our understanding that the United Sates Government will participate fully in all stages of negotiations.

Sincerely yours,

For the Government of Israel:

M. Begin

Menachem Begin

For the Government of the Arab Republic of Egypt:

A. Sadat

Mohammed Anwar al-Sadat

Note: President Carter, upon receipt of the joint letter to him from President Sadat and Prime Minister Begin, added to the American and Israeli copies the notation:

"I have been informed that the expression 'West Bank' is understood by the Government of Israel to mean 'Judea and Samaria.'"

This notation is in accordance with similar procedures established at Camp David.[2]

APPENDIX VI
THE ISRAELI AUTONOMY MODEL
January 16, 1980

At the conclusion of the last Plenary meeting held at Mena House, Al-Giza, Egypt, on 19 December 1979 it was decided:

> The Plenary also approved the recommendation of the working group in its report that it proceed simultaneously to prepare for the Plenary's future consideration a proposed model for the Powers and Responsibilities to be exercised by the Self-Governing Authority (Administrative Council).

In accordance with this decision the Israeli Working Group has prepared a proposed model for full autonomy for Palestinian Arab inhabitants of Judea, Samaria and the Gaza District. In this model the Israeli party presents a draft of the proposed model of the powers and responsibilities and functions which the Administrative Council should have in accordance with the provisions of the Camp David Framework.

The Israeli team tried to express its thoughts through this draft model on the organizational concept of the Administrative Council and its administrative tools. In order to more easily convey our conception to

---

[2]Explanatory note with the original documents.

all the participants here, we have made intense and minute preparations and we have in fact prepared a graphic representation of the model. On this poster we have delineated the powers and responsibilities of the Administrative Council itself, its Chairman, and its essential functions and attributes. Also on this poster you will see a list of the Divisions of the Administrative Council, the Divisions which will fulfill the powers and responsibilities and functions on the Council.

The other posters depict, in detail, the suggested structure of each of the Divisions with details of all the various sections of each Division. We have attempted to provide the model in detail and to present it clearly by using graphic illustrations so as to express Israel's position and Israel's preparedness to ensure full autonomy for Palestinian Arab inhabitants of Judea, Samaria, and the Gaza District.

As we have said on numerous occasions, Israel sees three different categories of powers and responsibilities:

The first is that described in the model, and includes all the powers and responsibilities to be given to the Administrative Council. In our opinion, this model covers all those elements needed to ensure full autonomy for the Palestinian Arab inhabitants of Judea, Samaria and the Gaza District.

The second category includes Powers and Responsibilities which will be administered jointly and through co-operation, the so-called "shared powers" between Israel and the Administrative Council.

The third category includes those powers and responsibilities which will remain in Israel's authority, the so-called "residual" powers.

It should be clear before presenting the detailed review that this is a draft, a proposed model, of the Israeli party to the negotiation. Not every detail of it is of crucial importance. We know that we have to shape together the final form of the proposed model we were requested to prepare by the plenary, but we were also requested, as we are the nearest to the problem, after we gave a presentation of the current situation, to prepare also a draft for the model and I believe that all of us can afterwards relate to it.

1. The Administrative Council will be composed of 11 members, a Chairman and 10 members each of whom will be Head of a Division.

General Powers of the Administrative Council

2. (a) The Administrative Council will have the following general powers:
    (i) The power to issue regulations;
    (ii)The power to determine the budget and mode of financing of the Administrative Council;
    (iii) The power to enter into contracts;
    (iv)The power to sue and be sued in the local courts;
    (v) The power to employ personnel.
  (b) The Administrative Council will be entitled to delegate all or part of its powers to the heads of Divisions functioning within its frame.

Divisions of the Administrative Council

3. The following Divisions will function within the frame of the Council:
Agriculture, Health, Religious, Labour and Welfare, Industry and Commerce, Finance, Transport and Communications, Education and Culture, Administration of Justice and Local Affairs (including Police).

4. *The Agriculture Division* will deal with all branches of agriculture and fisheries and with nature reserves and parks.

5. *The Health Division* will supervise the hospitals, clinics, and other health and sanitary services.

6. *The Religious Division* will deal with matters of religious services to all religious communities.

7. *The Labour and Welfare Division* will be responsible for the welfare, labour and employment services including the operation of labour exchanges, and will be responsible for the rehabilitation of refugees.

8. *The Industry and Commerce Division* will be responsible for all branches of commerce, industry and workshops.

9. *The Finance Division* will deal with the budget of the Administrative Council and its distribution among the various divisions, and will be responsible for matters of direct taxation.

10. *The Transport and Communications Division* will co-ordinate matters of transport, road traffic, meteorology, shipping and ports, and will be responsible for post and communications services.

11. *The Education and Culture Division* will operate the local system of educational institutions from kindergarten to institutions of higher education and will supervise cultural, art and sports activities.

12. *The Administration of Justice Division* will supervise the administrative system of the local courts, and will also deal with matters of the prosecution framework and with all matters of registration and association under the law (such as: companies, partnerships, patents, trademarks, etc.)

13. *The Local Affairs Division* will deal with matters of housing and construction inclusive of building licences, matters of local authorities, tourism and will be responsible for the operation of the local police force, including prisons for criminal offenders sentenced by the local courts.

14. *Each Division of the Administrative Council* will be managed by its own Director-General who will have under his jurisdiction special

assistants and section directors. The following sections will function in each of the Divisions:

(a) The Administration Section will deal with organization and management of the Division, employee affairs, budgets, finances and internal audit of the Division and its sections. The section will also be responsible for training and professional up-grading for employees of the Division.

(b) The Legal Department of each Division will provide legal advice to the Head of the Division, the Director-General, his assistants and the sections.

The Chairman of the Administrative Council will be responsible for coordinating the operations of the various Divisions of the Council. In addition, there will be in his office a number of non-elected functionaries appointed by the Chairman of the Council, as follows:

(a) The Statistics Section will be responsible for planning, collection, processing and publication of data in the form of surveys as, for example, on the following: population, labour force, wages and employment, consumption and standard of living, agriculture, industry and workshops, building, transportation, prices, etc.

(b) The Civil Service Commissioner will be responsible for employees of the Administrative Council in the following matters:

  (i)   Establishment for the Council's Divisions;
  (ii) Salaries and terms of employment;
  (iii) Employing and dismissing workers;
  (iv) Ongoing handling of all employee affairs.

This section will, *inter alia,* supervise work and organizational arrangements of the employees, will define their powers, their duties, their rights and obligations.

(c) The Official Publications Section will plan, carry out and publish the official publications of the Administrative Council and the various Divisions. Thus, for example, the Section will publish regulations issued by the Council and the by-laws of the local authorities, the various announcements of Divisions of the council, such as trademarks, patents, designs, companies, etc.

(d) The Archives will be responsible for the following areas:

  (i)   Collection of archive material from meetings of the Council and its Divisions, and the preservation thereof to the extent that its legal, administrative and research value so justifies.

  (ii) The opening of protected material for research by means of cataloguing and publication.

  (iii) Professional supervision in order that they should be properly kept.

  (iv) Destruction of archive material held by private individuals and public institutions and which is of concern to the population at large.

The following will function alongside the Chairman's Office: the Legal Adviser, Ombudsman and Comptroller of the Administrative Council.

(a) The Legal Adviser will provide legal advice to the Council and its Divisions in all matters arising from its ongoing functions, and guidance on future affairs. Within its responsibility will also be the regulatory system under the powers of the Council: preparation, drafting and co-ordination of regulations. The Legal Department will also be responsible for the function of the legal departments within each Division.

(b) The Ombudsman will deal with all requests submitted to the Chairman of the Council or directly to him, and which relate to matters where regular channels cannot provide satisfactory answers. The Ombudsman will deal with all requests relating to: administrative methods, regulations, attitudes of officials and the establishment—whether himself or by causing speedier handling by the Divisions concerned.

(c) The Comptroller will audit the activities of the various Divisions, and of the institutions connected with them: local authorities, legal entities in the management of which the Council participates or which it supports. The activities that he will audit are: functions according to law and regulations, public ethics, regular and efficient working and economies.

The Council Secretary will be responsible, under the direction of the Chairman, for preparing the agenda and other material connected with Council meetings, for relaying resolutions taken and for supervising their implementation. He will also be responsible for the functioning of those sections that operate in the frame of the Chairman's Office.

The Coordinator of Divisional Activities, alongside the Secretary, will coordinate activities between the Divisions whenever this is necessary in order to implement Council decisions.

Two separate representatives will operate in liaison roles:

(a) Liaison with the Continuing Committee in accordance with Article 3 of the Camp David Framework.

(b) Liaison Representative with the Israeli Authorities who will deal together with Israeli Authorities on an ongoing basis with all matters of common interest to the Council and Israel. This representative will also be responsible for coordination of all matters that require coordination according to the model to be presented.

APPENDIX VII
EGYPTIAN AUTONOMY MODEL
January 29, 1980

PREAMBLE

(A) The Camp David Framework for peace provides for the withdrawal of the Israeli Military Government and its Civil Administration and for the transfer of its powers to the Autonomy Authority that is to replace it.

(B) By reviewing the powers and responsibilities of the Military Government and its Civil Administration, the Working Group examined in a practical manner the powers and responsibilities to be assumed by the Autonomy Authority when it replaces the Military Government and its Civil Administration in accordance with the provisions of the Camp David Framework.

This has been the aim of the review of the current situation, as a means to break the deadlock resulting from the method used at the beginning in the comprehensive discussion of all the principles. It has also been a step to furnish the parties with the basic information necessary for discussing the transfer of authority.

In fact, the review of the powers and responsibilities of the Military Government and its Civil Administration was meant to guide the Working Group, in the light of the review and with regard to the transfer of authority, in preparing the pattern of powers and responsibilities to be assumed by the Autonomy Authority.

During their meeting in London on 26 October 1979, the delegation heads approved this method and decided on the following:

The review of the situation currently prevailing will furnish the parties with the basic information that will enable them to discuss the transfer of authority in the manner stipulated in the Camp David Framework–a point which subsequently led to the general committee's 19 December 1979 invitation to the Working Group to prepare a proposed pattern of the powers and responsibilities to be assumed by the Autonomy Authority and to submit it to the general committee for consideration.

(C) Having defined the procedure in this manner, it becomes clear that in drawing up the pattern of powers and responsibilities of the Autonomy Authority, the guideline must be the powers and responsibilities of the Military Government and its Civil Administration. The basic points for the discussion of this pattern should be:

(1) The withdrawal of the Israeli Military Government and its Civil Administration.

(2) The transfer of authority.

(3) The autonomy organs that are to take over authority from and replace the Military Government and its Civil Administration.

THE GOVERNMENT AND ITS CIVIL-MILITARY ADMINISTRATION

(A) On 7 June 1967, the Israeli Military Governor published Declaration No. 2 under the title: "A declaration on Law and Administration," part of which dealt with the assumption of government by the Israeli Defense Forces and which, under the "assumption of powers" clause, stipulated:

> All Government powers, legislation, appointments and administration related to the region or its inhabitants shall from now onward be vested in me alone and shall be exercised by me or by a person appointed by me or acting on my behalf.

(B) The Israeli Military Government existing in the West Bank and Gaza sector has comprehensive, full powers. It exercises the authority of drawing up all policies and coordinating all activities. Government decision making is achieved through various channels and linked with the Israeli Council of Minsters and on various ministerial levels, in addition to a series of military commands down to the area commander or the resident commander (the commander of the West Bank and the commander of Gaza sector), who is vested in his area with full legislative and executive powers in the manner shown in the previous paragraph.

Through military orders, the Military Governor issues new legislative degrees and amendments to existing laws. Policy is defined on the basis of consideration by the activities co-ordination office, the Israeli Ministry concerned and the area commander.

(C) Administrative power is mandated to the provincial and district leaders, and routine administrative tasks and the management of normal activities are left to the institutions concerned which are already actually carrying them out in the West Bank and Gaza, as well as to the new administrative units for services.

The Civil Administration of the Military Government consists of branches, each of which supervises a number of units which in turn manage the affairs of daily life.

Unit chiefs, through branch chiefs, come directly under the Military Governor and simultaneously, in technical matters, under the Ministries concerned, from which they receive instructions on how to act on those matters and how to deal with daily problems arising. They also receive from the Military Governor, through the branch chief, political guidance and executive power.

(D) Consequently, the Military Government and its Civil Administration consist of various levels exercising varying degrees of power, one legislating and laying down policies and the other executing and applying the policies.

The Camp David Framework has provided for the transfer of both types. The matter does not concern the transfer of the administrative structure that conveys orders, but of the authority which has the power to issue orders.

(E) It is worth noting that the Civil Administration of the Military Government basically consists even to this day of Palestinians.

According to a December 1978 survey there were 11,165 Palestinian employees in the West Bank Civil Administration and only 980 Israelis. In Gaza there are 14 basic units headed by Palestinian Directors-General.

It can therefore be said that up to the present time the Palestinians have been taking most of the responsibilities of managing their daily affairs but were implementing decisions made for them and carrying out policies shaped by others.

Therefore, when the Camp David Framework promises them full autonomy, this can only mean that under the Autonomy Authority they will be able to make their own decisions and shape their own policies.

The full autonomy provided for in the Camp David Framework for peace might appear to be merely a reorganization of what the Palestinians in the West Bank and Gaza actually have, whereas naturally it must be dedicated to the complete formation of the Autonomy Authority itself and to the withdrawal of the Military Government and the transfer of its various powers to the inhabitants.

WITHDRAWAL OF THE MILITARY GOVERNMENT AND THE TRANSFER OF POWER

(A) The first step to the establishment of autonomy must be the withdrawal of the Military Government. The Camp David Framework for peace clearly provided for the following:

> The Military Government and its Civil Administration shall withdraw as soon as the inhabitants of these areas freely elect the Autonomy Authority that will replace the existing Military Government.

The supplementary agreement dated March 26, 1979 provided the following:

> The Military Government and its Civil Administration shall withdraw in order to be replaced by the Autonomy Authority.

(B) The Camp David Framework and the supplementary agreement both differentiated between the types of withdrawal in letters exchanged about withdrawal:

First: The withdrawal of the Military Government and its Civil Administration, which should be total and absolute.

Second: Withdrawal of the Israeli military forces, which shall be partial, with the remaining forces being redeployed in specific security areas.

(C) The withdrawal of the Military Government and its Civil Administration, which will take place as soon as an Autonomy Authority is elected, is the first step for this authority, to assume its powers and responsibilities. The transfer of power takes place by the Military Government and its Civil Administration transferring their powers and responsibilities to the newly elected Authority.

Thus the self-rule authority will replace the old regime.

(D) In this regard the following factors must be underlined:

(1) The transfer of power means the handing over of all the powers and responsibilities exercised by the Military Government and its Administration.

(2) The transfer of power should be carried out in a peaceful and organized manner.

(3) If, during the process of transfer of power, a Palestinian organ is found which is part of the existing local administration in the West Bank and Gaza, it may assume the powers of and replace the Military Government and its Civil Administration. But if new responsibilities or powers are to be transferred to the Autonomy Authority which were not previously exercised by the Palestinians under the military rule, a search for new organs must be pursued.

(E) Powers and responsibilities that were not previously exercised by Palestinians under the military rule must be determined with a view to proposing the necessary organs required for this.

The Palestinians have played the major role in the Civil Administration which carried out the policies and orders issued by the military regime. But under the autonomy regime it is necessary to create a new organ to exercise the new powers, make its own decisions and draw up its own policies. There is no doubt that the elected Autonomy Authority will be this organ.

THE POWERS AND RESPONSIBILITIES EXERCISED BY THE AUTONOMY AUTHORITY

In order to determine the type of powers and responsibilities exercised by the Autonomy Authority, certain terms in the provisions of the Camp David Framework for peace considered to be the key and the guide must be underlined from the beginning:

(A) It is an Autonomy Authority in the sense that it rules itself by itself and exercises its powers from within. No outside source shall impose its authority on it.

(B) It shall prepare full, not partial or incomplete self-rule.

(C) It shall come about as a result of free elections, which will make it a democratic ruling authority for the people and by the people. Since it is an elected body, it is of a representative character and exercises all the responsibilities and powers that are usually exercised by an elected power.

CHARACTERISTICS OF THE AUTONOMY AUTHORITY

The Autonomy Authority is considered a temporary arrangement for a transitional period not exceeding five years. This transition, whose beginning is the withdrawal of the Military Government and its Civil Administration and the establishment of the Autonomy Authority, may prove that the practical problems of progress toward peace can be solved satisfactorily. The transition period aims at change in attitudes that may lead to a final settlement which will achieve the legitimate rights of the Palestinian people and guarantee security for all the parties.

The purpose of these transitional arrangements is:

(A) To ensure the transfer of authority to the Palestinian people in the West Bank and Gaza sector in a peaceful and organized manner.

(B) To help the Palestinian people to develop their political, economic and social institutions in the West Bank and Gaza sector in order to achieve the principle of full autonomy provided by the indigenous authority.

(C) To create suitable conditions for the Palestinian people to participate in the negotiations that will lead to the solution of the Palestinian problem in all its aspects and to the attainment of the Palestinian people's lawful rights, including their right to self-determination.

THE EXTENT OF THE AUTONOMY AUTHORITY

(A) The Autonomy Authority shall extend over all the Palestinian areas which were occupied after 5 June 1967 and which were defined in the 1949 Armistice Agreements (the 2 April 1949 Egyptian-Israeli Armistice Agreement regarding the Gaza sector and the 24 February 1949 Jordanian-Israeli Armistice Agreement regarding the West Bank, including Arab Jerusalem).

(B) The Autonomy Authority in the West Bank and Gaza sector shall extend over both the inhabitants and the land alike.

(C) All the Autonomy powers and responsibilities shall apply to the West Bank and Gaza sector, which will be considered as one region under full autonomy.

(D) All changes made in the geographical nature, the demographic structure or the legal status of all or part of the West Bank and Gaza sector shall be considered null and void and must be abolished because they obstruct the attainment of the Palestinian people's lawful rights as defined in the Camp David Framework for peace, particularly with regard to the following:

(1) The Israeli decision to annex East Jerusalem is considered null and void and must be abolished. The SC resolutions in this connection must be applied, particularly Resolutions 242 and 267 on Jerusalem, which is an indivisible part of the West Bank. The Arab legal and historical rights to the city must be respected and restored.

(2) The Israeli settlements in the West Bank and Gaza sector are illegal and, within the framework of a final settlement, must be withdrawn (*sahbaha*). An end must also be put to the building of new settlements and to the expansion of the existing settlements during the transitional period. On the establishment of the Autonomy Authority, all the settlements and settlers in the West Bank and Gaza sector shall come under its authority.

GENERAL POWERS AND RESPONSIBILITIES OF THE AUTONOMOUS AUTHORITY

(A) The promulgation of laws and regulations.

(B) The charting of policies and the monitoring of their implementation.

(C) The preparation and approval of the budget.

(D) The levying and collection of taxes.

(E) The appointment of individual officials.

(F) The issue of identity cards and travel documents.

(G) Control of the entry and exit of individuals and goods to and from the region.

(H) The competence to assume commitments and ownership.

(I) The power to own public land.

(J) The power to adjudicate.

(K) The power to ratify contracts.

(L) The power to participate in the final negotiations on defining the final status of the West Bank and Gaza sector and to seek the opinion of the Palestinians.

(M) The following responsibilities: public administration; public services; internal security, public order and police; public property and natural resources; economic and financial fields; social and cultural fields; respect for human rights and public freedoms;

(N) Judicial authority and law enforcement.

STRUCTURE OF THE AUTONOMY AUTHORITY

(A) The Autonomy Authority shall consist of 80 to 100 members to be freely elected by the Palestinian people in the West Bank and Gaza sector.

(B) The structure of the Autonomy Authority shall consist of two institutions:

A Parliamentary Assembly comprising all those freely elected as representatives of the West Bank and Gaza sector:

An Executive Council comprising of 10 to 15 members to be elected by the Parliamentary Assembly.

(C)   The Parliamentary Assembly:

(1) The Parliamentary Assembly assumes the powers of and replaces the Military Government in legislating laws and by-laws, drawing up policies, supervising their implementation, approving the budget, levying taxes and so on and so forth.

(2)   The Assembly decides its statues by itself. It also decides the formation of its Presidium, which is to comprise its Speaker and one or more of his Deputies and the number and formation of its internal committee.

(D) The Executive Council:

(1) The Executive Council assumes the actual administration of the West Bank and Gaza and implements the policies drawn up by the Parliamentary Assembly in the various fields.

(2)   It shall have comprehensive powers in all the spheres and have absolute jurisdiction to organize, administer, appoint individual officials and supervise the following branches: Education, Culture and Information, Health, Transport and Communications, Social Affairs, Labour, Tourism, Internal Security, Housing, Religious Affairs, Agriculture, Economic Affairs, Finance and Trade, Industry and Justice.

(E) The Council shall establish its own departments and branches as it may deem necessary for the proper conduct of its tasks. It shall determine the number of the departments and their internal organizations and the machinery of co-ordination between them as may be required for the best and most effective performance to achieve its activities. It may in this regard seek expert assistance from other parties.

(F) The organization of the judiciary shall be achieved through a system of Courts, a Court of Appeal and a Higher court and the ensuring of full guarantees for the independence of the judiciary and its proper administration of justice.

(G) The Autonomy Authority shall have a representative alongside representatives from Israel and Egypt (and Jordan) at the permanent committee emanating from the Camp David Framework for peace (Article 2). All matters of interest to Israel and to the Autonomy

Authority that need a common solution may be solved through the said committee.

HEADQUARTERS OF THE AUTONOMY AUTHORITY

The headquarters of the Autonomy Authority shall be in East Jerusalem.

Additional Arrangements

(A) Immediately upon the establishment of the Autonomy Authority in the West Bank and Gaza sector the Israeli armed forces shall withdraw and the remaining forces shall be redeployed to specified security positions. Any move by the military forces to or through the region requires permission.

(B) The Camp David Framework for peace provides for negotiations to be held between the parties for an agreement that provides, among other things, for determining arrangements to insure internal and external security and public-order.

Responsibility for security and public order shall be determined collectively by the parties, which include the Palestinians, Israelis, Egyptians (and Jordanians). The US will participate fully in this settlement.

(C) A strong local police force shall be established in the West Bank and Gaza Sector. It shall be established by the Autonomy Authority and consist of the inhabitants of the West Bank and Gaza sector.

(D) A land route is to be established between the West Bank and Gaza sector, and agreement is to be reached on the arrangements for linking the two areas.

APPENDIX VIII
LINOWITZ REPORT[3]
January 14, 1981

Dear Mr. President:

I am pleased to submit to you these two brief reports—one summarizing the progress thus far made in the Autonomy neogtiations and the other the developments in the Egyptian-Israeli normalization process. These reports reflect my experience in the area over the past year and take into account my consultations with President Sadat and Prime Minister Begin.

As you know, during my December visit both leaders agreed that important progress had been made in the negotiations toward realization of the objectives of the Camp David Accords and they expressed their confidence that they would be able fully to fulfill the promise of Camp David.

President Sadat and Prime Minister Begin also affirmed their strong conviction that the process which you had developed with them at Camp david is, in their words, "the only viable path toward comprehensible peace in the Middle East today." I share that conviction and deeply believe that it is in the highest interest of the United States to press forward in the weeks and months ahead in order to conclude the negotiations at the earliest possible date.

I have been honored to serve as your representative in these negotiations.

Respectively submitted,

Sol M. Linowitz
Personal Representative of the
President for the Middle East
Peace Negotiations

PROGRESS IN THE AUTONOMY NEGOTIATIONS

Egypt and Israel have over the past months, by virtue of their commitment and efforts, been able to make considerable progress and have appreciably narrowed their differences on a wide range of critical, substantive matters germane to the concept of "full autonomy" called for by the Camp David Accords.

While significant differences remain on important issues which will require extensive and intensive negotiations during the weeks and

---

[3]Submitted to President Carter by Sol M. Linowitz, Personal Representative of the President for the Middle East Peace Negotiations. The letter and the portion of the report dealing with autonomy are printed here.

months ahead, it can fairly be said that a substantial consensus now exists between the parties on the elements set forth below.

This report undertakes to reflect in general terms the extent to which the parties are in accord although they have not agreed on the precise language used to express this consensus in all cases. Each of the parties has emphasized that its position on a number of these matters is expressly conditioned on the completion of a comprehensive autonomy agreement. In addition, Egypt has consistently maintained that in a number of areas it has no mandate to agree to detailed provisions that will bind the inhabitants of the territories in the absence of their participation. Nevertheless, the existing consensus as reflected below provides a solid foundation for the completion of a comprehensive agreement which will establish the transitional autonomy arrangements contemplated in the Accords.

1. *Election of Self-Governing Authority*

As provided in the Camp David Accords the inhabitants of the territories would elect a self-governing authority (administrative council) "SGA (AC)." The SGA (AC) would select its own officers from among the elected members and determine its own internal procedures.

Proposals have been made by both parties on the SGA (AC)'s size and structure, and some progress in narrowing the differences has been made. The parties are proceeding on the basis that these issues can be more appropriately resolved once the scope and nature of the SGA (AC)'s powers and responsibilities have been more fully defined.

As called for by the Camp David Accords and the joint letter of March 26, 1979, the SGA (AC) would be established and inaugurated within one month after it has been elected, at which time the transitional period of five years would begin. The Israeli military government and its civilian administration would be withdrawn, to be replaced by the SGA (AC) as specified in the "Framework for Peace in the Middle East." A withdrawal of Israeli armed forces would then take place and there would be a redeployment of the remaining Israeli forces into specified security locations.

The parties are agreed that there must be free elections based on the principles of peaceful assembly, free expression and secret ballot, bearing in mind the need to preserve law and order. Free electoral campaigning will be guaranteed in accordance with the agreement on election modalities which has now been virtually completed. The parties have not yet selected a system for apportioning representation because of their strong differences over the issue of participation by Palestinian inhabitants of Jerusalem.

The election would be organized, conducted and supervised by a Central Electoral Commission, composed of authorized Israeli civilian personnel and local Palestinian Arabs agreed upon by the autonomy negotiators, together with other civilians–individual and institutional–as agreed upon by the negotiators. There will be free access for international media and for such experts as may be agreed upon by the parties.

2. *Powers and Responsibilities of the SGA (AC)*

Contingent upon full agreement on defining the structure and the powers and responsibilities of the SGA (AC) the parties in the negotiating process have agreed upon at least the following areas and functions with respect to which the SGA (AC) would exercise responsibility:

> Administration of Justice
> Agriculture
> Budget
> Civil Service
> Commerce
> Culture
> Ecology
> Education
> Finance
> Health
> Housing and Construction
> Industry
> Internal Communication and Posts
> Internal Transportation
> Labor
> Local Police and Prisons
> Manpower
> Municipal Affairs
> Nature Preserves and Parks
> Public Works
> Religious Affairs
> Refugee Rehabilitation
> Social Welfare
> Taxation
> Tourism

Other areas and functions in which the SGA (AC) would exercise responsibility are under discussion and negotiation.

The parties anticipate that the SGA (AC) would have the powers necessary and appropriate to the exercise of its agreed responsibilities. That would include, among others, the power to decide upon the budget and determine the means of financing it to employ staff; to sue and be sued; to enter into contracts, etc.

Considerable attention has been devoted to defining the nature of the legislative power appropriate for the SGA (AC). While some differences remain on this issue, the parties have made significant progress. Both would agree that the SGA (AC) must be empowered to promulgate such measure as are necessary to the proper fulfillment of its responsibilities under full autonomy. It is expected that the exercise of power would be limited to the defined responsibilities, would not impinge on issues reserved for resolution in the final status negotiations, and must be consistent with the transitional nature of the arrangement and the security provisions and mechanisms called for by the Framework.

In reaching agreement on the above powers and responsibilities, it has been understood that, in the interests of all affected parties, coordination between the SGA (AC) and Israel will be necessary in some specifically defined areas. Mechanisms to achieve this end must be worked out in the course of the negotiations.

In connection with the issue of land, it is intended that lawful private ownership of land in the territories not be impaired during the transitional period. As to public lands, determination of their ultimate status and uses must be addressed in the final status negotiations. While extensive negotiations will still be required, proposals have recently been made by the parties which may offer a basis for resolving the problem of public land and Israeli settlements during the transitional period.

As to water, the parties have put forth proposals dealing with arrangements for the transitional period and the gap between them has been narrowed. In developing these arrangements the parties would undertake to ensure that the mechanisms instituted for new development and use of water resources would not adversely affect the inhabitants of the territories or Israel. They would also agree that both the inhabitants and Israel share an essential stake in the disposition of those water resources which underlie both the territories and Israel and to that end coordination between them will be necessary. Both parties might favor the establishment of a regional body representing the various peoples of the area in order to develop and use the water resources for the benefit of all those peoples.

In connection with security, it is agreed that the inhabitants of both the territories and Israel require assured internal security and public order during the transitional period. Accordingly, it is recognized that the strong local police force, to be constituted by the SGA (AC), must help provide such security. Specific arrangements for liaison between the local police and Israeli security authorities on such security issues, as called for in the Camp David Framework, will be worked out in the course of the negotiations and will be implemented in such a way as to ensure that security is preserved.

To assure external security, and in the absence of Jordanian participation as envisioned in the Camp David Framework, the responsibility for external security set forth in the Framework would logically fall to Israel. The precise arrangements remain to be specified and further elaboration will be sought on how to enable Israel to fulfill fully its responsibilities while minimizing the impact on the inhabitants.

The parties plan the establishment of a Continuing Committee with Egypt, Israel and the SGA (AC) as members (Jordan has, of course, the option of joining under the provision of the Framework), and with the United States also invited to participate. The Committee would decide by agreement on the modalities of admission of persons displaced in 1967, together with measures necessary to prevent disruption and disorder. The Committee would also deal with other matters of common concern, such as economic cooperation.

As you know so well, troublesome problems still remain to be resolved and difficult negotiations still lie ahead. It is significant, however, that on December 13, 1980 President Sadat and Prime Minister Begin together issued a statement reaffirming their commitment to the Camp David peace process as "the only viable path toward comprehensive peace in the Middle East today."

With the determined efforts of all parties and with continued active participation on the part of the United States, I firmly believe that the current negotiations can be successfully concluded, thereby providing the foundation for resolution of the Palestinian problem in all its aspects and for comprehensive peace with security for Israel and all the peoples of the Middle East.

APPENDIX IX
ISRAEL'S FINAL AUTONOMY PROPOSAL
January, 1982

In the Camp David Agreement signed on 17 September 1978 between Egypt and Israel, with the United States signing as a witness, agreement was reached on a plan for the solution of the problem of the Palestinian Arabs, that includes a proposal for full autonomy for the Palestinian Arabs living in Judea-Samaria and Gaza. The manner of establishing this autonomy, as well as its powers, were to be determined in negotiations between the signatories (Jordan was invited to participate, but did not respond). It was Israel that first raised the idea of autonomy that was later to serve as the basis of the Camp David agreement. For the first time in the history of the Palestinian Arab inhabitants of Judea-Samaria and the Gaza District, they were offered an opportunity of this kind to conduct their own affairs by themselves. Since 1979, talks have been held for the implementation of this agreement; there were intermissions in the negotiations, but talks were resumed intensively in the summer of 1981, leading to a thoroughgoing clarification of the positions of the parties. At these talks Israel put forward its proposals with regard to the self-governing authority administrative council), its powers, responsibilities and structure as well as other related issues. The main points of Israel's proposals, as submitted in the course of the negotiations were as follows:

SCOPE, JURISDICTION AND STRUCTURE OF THE SELF-GOVERNING AUTHORITY (ADMINISTRATIVE COUNCIL):

1. The Camp David accords set forth the establishment of a self-governing authority (administrative council) that will comprise one body representing the Arab inhabitants of Judea, Samaria, and the Gaza District, who will choose this body in free elections, and it will assume those functional powers that will be transferred to it. Thus the Palestinians Arabs will for the first time have an elected and representative body, in accordance with their own wishes and free

choice, that will be able to carry out the functions assigned to it as an administrative council.

2. The members of the administrative council will be able, as a group, to discuss all subjects within the council's competence, apportioning among themselves the spheres of responsibility for the various functions. Within the domain of its assigned powers and responsibilities, the council will be responsible for planning and carrying out its activities.

POWERS OF THE SELF-GOVERNING AUTHORITY (ADMINISTRATIVE COUNCIL):

1. (a) Under the terms of the Camp David agreement, the parties have to reach an agreement on the powers and responsibilities of the authority. Israel's detailed proposals include a list of powers that will be given to the authority and that, by any reasonable and objective criterion, represent a wide and comprehensive range of field of operation. Without any doubt, the transferring of these powers constitutes the bestowal of full autonomy–in the full meaning of that term.

(b) The powers to be granted the authority, under these proposals, are in the following domains:

1. *Administration of Justice:* Supervision of the administrative system of the courts in the areas; dealing with matters connected with the prosecution system and with the registration of companies, partnerships, patents, trademarks, etc.

2. *Agriculture:* All branches of agriculture and fisheries, nature reserves and parks.

3. *Finance:* Budget of the administrative council and allocations among its various divisions; taxation.

4. *Civil Service:* Appointment and working conditions of the Council's employees. (Today, the civil service of the inhabitants of Judea, Samaria and Gaza, within the framework of the Military Government's Civilian Administration, numbers about 12,000 persons.)

5. *Education and Culture:* Operation of the network of schools in the areas, from kindergarten to higher education; supervision of cultural, artistic and sporting activities.

6. *Health:* Supervision of hospitals and clinics; operation of sanitary and other services related to public health.

7. *Housing and Public Works:* Construction, housing for the inhabitants and public works projects.

8. *Transportation and Communications:* Maintenance and coordination of transport, road traffic, meteorology; local postal and communications services.

9. *Labour and Social Welfare:* Welfare, labour and employment services, including the operation of labour exchanges.

10. *Municipal Affairs:* Matters concerning municipalities and their effective operation.

11. *Local Police:* Operation of a strong local police force, as provided for in the Camp David agreement, and maintenance of prisons for criminal offenders sentenced by the courts in the areas.

12. *Religious Affairs:* Provision and maintenance of religious facilities for all religious communities among the Arab inhabitants of Judea-Samaria and the Gaza District.

13. *Industry, Commerce, and Tourism:* Development of industry, commerce, workshops and tourist services.

2. The council will have full powers in its spheres of competence to determine its budget, to enter into contractual obligations, to sue and be sued and to engage manpower. It will, moreover, have wide powers to promulgate regulations, as required by a body of this kind. In the nature of things, in view of the free movement that will prevail between Judea-Samaria and the Gaza District and Israel and for the general welfare of the inhabitants, arrangements will be agreed upon in the negotiations, in a number of domains, for cooperation and coordination with Israel. The administrative council will, hence, have full scope to exercise its wide-ranging powers under the terms of the autonomy agreement. These powers embrace all walks of life, and will enable the inhabitants the areas concerned to enjoy full autonomy.

3. Size: The size of the administrative council must reflect its functions and its essential purpose: it is an administrative council, whose representative character finds expression in its establishment through free elections, by the Arab inhabitants of Judea, Samaria and Gaza. Clearly, the criterion for determining the number of its members must be the functions that the council is empowered to perform. We propose, therefore, that the number of members will conform with the functions listed above.

4. Free Elections: Elections to the administrative council, under Israel's proposals, will be absolutely free, as stipulated in the Camp David agreement. Under the terms of the agreement, the parties will agree upon the modalities of the elections; as a matter of fact, in past negotiations a long list of principles and guidelines has already been prepared in this matter. In these free elections, all the rights pertaining to a peaceful assembly, freedom of expression and secret balloting will be

preserved and assured, and all necessary steps will be taken to prevent any interference with the election process. The holding of an absolutely free and unhampered election process will thus be assured in full, under the law, and in keeping with the tradition of free elections practiced in democratic societies. These elections will, in many respects, constitute a new departure in the region around us which in most of its parts is not too close to the ways of democracy, and in which free elections are a rare phenomenon. It is of some interest, therefore, to note that Judea-Samaria and Gaza, under Israel's Military Government since 1967, have exemplified the practical possibility of totally free elections in these areas. In 1972, and again in 1976, Israel organized free elections in these areas based on the tradition and model of its own democratic and liberal tradition and custom; voters and elected officials alike conceded that these were free elections in the fullest sense. The elections in the administrative council will be organized and supervised by a central elections committee whose composition has been agreed upon by the parties.

5. Time of elections and establishment of the self-governing authority (administrative council): The elections will be held as expeditiously as possible after agreement will have been reached on the autonomy. This was set forth in the joint letter of the late President Sadat and of Prime Minister Begin to President Carter, dated 26 March 1979, setting forth the manner in which the self-governing authority (administrative council) is to be established, under the terms of the Camp David agreement.

6. Within one month following the elections, the self-governing authority (administrative council) is to be established and inaugurated, and at that time the transitional period of five years will begin—again, in conformity with the Camp David agreement and the joint letter.

7. Hence, every effort will be made to hold elections without delay, once an agreement is reached, to be followed by the establishment of the self-governing authority (administrative council).

8. Following the elections and the establishment of the self-governing authority (administrative council) the military government and its civilian administration will be withdrawn, a withdrawal of Israeli armed forces will take place, and there will be a redeployment of the remaining Israeli forces into specified security locations, in full conformity with the Camp David agreement. Israel will present to the other parties in the negotiations the map of the specified security locations for the redeployment. It goes without saying that all this will be done for the purpose of safeguarding the security of Israel as well as of the Arab inhabitants of Judea-Samaria and Gaza and of the Israeli citizens residing in these areas.

9. All of the above indicates Israel's readiness to observe the Camp David agreement fully and in every detail, in letter and spirit, while safeguarding the interests of all concerned.

APPENDIX X
PRESIDENT RONALD REAGAN'S
TALKING POINTS SENT TO PRIME MINISTER BEGIN[4]
September 1, 1982

GENERAL PRINCIPLES

A. We will maintain our commitment to Camp David.

B. We will maintain our commitment to the conditions we require for recognition of and negotiation with the PLO.
C. We can offer guarantees on the position we will adopt in negotiations. We will not be able, however, to guarantee in advance the results of these negotiations.

TRANSITIONAL MEASURES

A. Our position is that the objective of the transitional period is the peaceful and orderly transfer of authority from Israel to the Palestinian inhabitants.

B. We will support:
—The decision of full autonomy as giving the Palestinian inhabitants real authority over themselves, the land and its resources, subject to fair safeguards on water.
—Economic, commercial, social and cultural ties between the West Bank, Gaza and Jordan.
—Participation by the Palestinian inhabitants of East Jerusalem in the election of the West Bank-Gaza authority.
—Real settlements freeze.
—Progressive Palestinian responsibility for internal security based on capability and performance.

---

[4]The talking points accompanied a letter sent by President Reagan to Prime Minister Menachem Begin of Israel. The same points were presented to Arab governments. See *The New York Times*, September 9, 1982.

C. We will oppose:
—Dismantlement of the existing settlements.
—Provisions which represent a legitimate threat to Israel's security, reasonably defined.
—Isolation of the West Bank and Gaza from Israel.
—Measures which accord either the Palestinians or the Israelis generally recognized sovereign rights with the exception of external security, which must remain in Israel's hands during the transitional period.

FINAL STATUS ISSUES

A. UNSC Resolution 242
It is our position that Resolution 242 applies to the West Bank and Gaza and requires Israeli withdrawal in return for peace. Negotiations must determine the borders. The U.S. position in these negotiations on the extent of the withdrawal will be significantly influenced by the extent and nature of the peace and security arrangements offered in return.

B. Israeli Sovereignty
It is our belief that the Palestinian problem cannot be resolved (through) Israeli sovereignty or control over the West Bank and Gaza. Accordingly, we will not support such a solution.

C. Palestinian State
The preference we will pursue in the final status negotiation is association of the West Bank and Gaza with Jordan. We will not support the formation of a Palestinian state in those negotiations. There is no foundation of political support in Israel or the United States for such a solution. The outcome, however, must be determined by negotiations.

D. Self-Determination
In the Middle East context the term self-determination has been identified exclusively with the formation of a Palestinian state. We will not support this definition of self-determination. We believe that the Palestinians must take the leading role in determining their own future and fully support the provision in Camp David providing for the elected representatives of the inhabitants of the West Bank and Gaza to decide how they shall govern themselves consistent with the provision of their agreement in the final status negotiations.

E. Jerusalem
We will fully support the position that the status of Jerusalem must be determined through negotiations.

F. Settlements

The status of Israeli settlements must be determined in the course of the final status negotiations. We will not support their continuation as extraterritorial outposts.

ADDITIONAL TALKING POINTS

1. Approach to Hussein

—The President has approached Hussein to determine the extent to which he may be interested in participating.

—King Hussein has received the same U.S. positions as you.

—Hussein considers our proposals serious and gives them serious attention.

—Hussein understands that Camp David is the only base that we will accept for negotiations.

—We are also discussing these proposals with the Saudis.

2. Public Commitment

—Whatever the support from these or other Arab States, this is what the President has concluded must be done.

—The President is convinced his positions are fair and balanced and fully protective of Israel's security. Beyond that they offer the practical opportunity of eventually achieving the peace treaties Israel must have with its neighbors.

—He will be making a speech announcing these positions, probably within a week.

3. Next Procedural Steps

—Should the response to the President's proposal be positive, the U.S. would take immediate steps to relaunch the autonomy negotiations with the broadest possible participation as envisaged under the Camp David agreements.

—We also contemplate an early visit by Secretary Shultz in the area.

—Should there not be a positive response, the President, as he has said in his letter to you, will nonetheless stand by his position with proper dedication.

APPENDIX XI
REAGAN PEACE INITIATIVE[5]
September 1, 1982

First, as outlined in the Camp David accords, there must be a period of time during which the Palestinian inhabitants of the West Bank and Gaza will have full autonomy over their own affairs. Due consideration must be given to the principle of self-government by the inhabitants of the territories and to the legitimate security concerns of the parties involved.

The purpose of the 5-year period of transition, which would begin after free elections for a self-governing Palestinian authority, is to prove to the Palestinians that they can run their own affairs and that such Palestinian autonomy poses no threat to Israel's security.

The United States will not support the use of any additional land for the purpose of settlements during the transition period. Indeed, the immediate adoption of a settlement freeze by Israel, more than any other action, could create the confidence needed for wider participation in these talks. Further settlement activity is in no way necessary for the security of Israel and only diminishes the confidence of the Arabs that a final outcome can be freely and fairly negotiated.

I want to make the American position well understood: The purpose of this transition period is the peaceful and orderly transfer of authority from Israel to the Palestinian inhabitants of the West Bank and Gaza. At the same time, such a transfer must not interfere with Israel's security requirements.

Beyond the transition period, as we look to the future of the West Bank and Gaza, it is clear to me that peace cannot be achieved by the formation of an independent Palestinian state in those territories. Nor is it achievable on the basis of Israeli sovereignty or permanent control over the West Bank and Gaza.

So the United States will not support the establishment of an independent Palestinian state in the West Bank and we will not support annexation or permanent control by Israel.

There is, however, another way to peace. The final status of these lands must, of course, be reached through the give-and-take of negotiations. But it is the firm view of the United States that self-government by the Palestinians of the West Bank and Gaza in association with Jordan offers the best chance for a durable, just and lasting peace.

We base our approach squarely on the principle that the Arab-Israeli conflict should be resolved through negotiation involving an exchange of

---

[5]Following the Israeli invasion of Lebanon in June 1982, the United States attempted to continue the Camp David peace process. On September 1, 1982, President Ronald Reagan presented the following proposal.

territory for peace. This exchange is enshrined in UN Security Council Resolution 242, which is, in turn, incorporated in all its parts in the Camp David agreements. UN Resolution 242 remains wholly valid as the foundation stone of America's Middle East peace effort.

It is the United States' position that—in return for peace—the withdrawal provision of Resolution 242 applies to all fronts, including the West Bank and Gaza.

When the border is negotiated between Jordan and Israel, our view on the extent to which Israel should be asked to give up territory will be heavily affected by the extent of true peace and normalization and the security arrangements offered in return.

Finally, we remain convinced that Jerusalem must remain undivided, but its final status should be decided through negotiations.

In the course of the negotiations to come, the United States will support positions that seem to us fair and reasonable compromises and likely to promote a sound agreement. We will also put forward our own detailed proposals when we believe they can be helpful. And, make no mistake, the United States will oppose any proposal—from any party and at any point in the negotiating process—that threatens the security of Israel. America's commitment to the security of Israel is ironclad. And, I might add, so is mine.

APPENDIX XII
PERES-HUSSEIN AGREEMENT
(THE LONDON DOCUMENT)[6]
April 11, 1987

(Accord between the Government of Jordan, which has confirmed it to the Government of the United States, and the Foreign Minister of Israel, pending the approval of the Government of Israel. Parts "A" and "B," which will be made public upon agreement of the parties, will be treated as proposals of the United States to which Jordan and Israel have agreed. Part "C" is to be treated with great confidentiality, as commitments to the United States from the Government of Jordan to be transmitted to the Government of Israel.)

---

[6]The London document was agreed to by Peres and Hussein in their meeting in London in April 1987. See *Ma'ariv*, January 1, 1988 in Foreign Broadcast Information Service, Daily Report: Near East and South Asia, January 4, 1988, pp. 30-31.

A THREE-PART UNDERSTANDING BETWEEN JORDAN AND ISRAEL

A. Invitation by the UN secretary general: the UN secretary general will send invitations to the five permanent members of the Security Council and to the parties involved in the Israeli-Arab conflict to negotiate an agreement by peaceful means based on UN Resolutions 242 and 338 with the purpose of attaining comprehensive peace in the region and security for the countries in the area, and granting the Palestinian people their legitimate rights.

B. Decisions of the international conference: The participants in the conference agree that the purpose of the negotiations is to attain by peaceful means an agreement about all the aspects of the Palestinian problem. The conference invites the sides to set up regional bilateral committees to negotiate bilateral issues.

C. Nature of the agreement between Jordan and Israel: Israel and Jordan agree that:

1) the international conference will not impose a solution and will not veto any agreement reached by the sides;

2) the negotiations will be conducted in bilateral committees in a direct manner;

3) the Palestinian issue will be discussed in a meeting of the Jordanian, Palestinian, and Israeli delegations;

4) the representatives of the Palestinians will be included in the Jordanian-Palestinian delegation;

5) participation in the conference will be based on acceptance of UN Resolutions 242 and 338 by the sides and the renunciation of violence and terror;

6) each committee will conduct negotiations independently;

7) other issues will be resolved through mutual agreement between Jordan and Israel.

This document of understanding is pending approval of the incumbent governments of Israel and Jordan. The content of this document will be presented and proposed to the United States.

APPENDIX XIII
PALESTINIAN "FOURTEEN POINTS" PROPOSAL[7]
January 14, 1988

During the past few weeks the occupied territories have witnessed a popular uprising against Israel's occupation and its oppressive measures. This uprising has so far resulted in the martyrdom of tens of our people, the wounding of hundreds more and the imprisonment of thousands of unarmed civilians.

This uprising has come to further affirm our people's unbreakable commitment to its national aspirations. These aspirations include our people's firm national rights of self-determination and of the establishment of an independent state on our national soil under the leadership of the PLO, as our sole legitimate representative. The uprising also comes as further proof of our indefatigable spirit and our rejection of the sense of despair which has begun to creep to the minds of some who claim that the uprising is the result of despair.

The conclusion to be drawn from this uprising is that the present state of affairs in the Palestinian occupied territories is unnatural and that Israeli occupation cannot continue forever. Real peace cannot be achieved except through the recognition of the Palestinian national rights, including the right of self-determination and the establishment of an independent Palestinian state on Palestinian national soil. Should these rights not be recognized, then the continuation of Israeli occupation will lead to further violence and bloodshed and the further deepening of hatred. The opportunity for achieving peace will also move further away.

The only way to extricate ourselves from this scenario is through the convening of an international conference with the participation of all concerned parties including the PLO, the sole legitimate representative of the Palestinian people, as an equal partner, as well as the five permanent members of the Security Council, under the supervision of the two Super Powers.

On this basis we call upon the Israeli authorities to comply with the following list of demands as a means to prepare the atmosphere for the convening of the suggested international peace conference which will achieve a just and lasting settlement of the Palestinian problem in all its aspects, bringing about the realization of the inalienable national rights of the Palestinian people, peace and stability for the peoples of the region and an end to violence and bloodshed:

1. To abide by the 4th Geneva Convention and all other international agreements pertaining to the protection of civilians, their properties and rights under a state of military occupation; to declare the Emergency Regulations of the British mandate null and void, and to stop applying the iron fist policy.

---

[7]Statement submitted to Secretary of State George Shultz by Hanna Siniora and Fayez Abu Rahme after the start of the *intifadah*.

2. The immediate compliance with Security Council Resolutions 605 and 607, which call upon Israel to abide by the Geneva convention of 1949 and the Declaration of Human Rights; and which further call for the achievement of a just and lasting settlement of the Arab-Israeli conflict.

3. The release of all prisoners who were arrested during the recent uprising, and foremost among them our children. Also the rescinding of all proceedings and indictments against them.

4. The cancellation of the policy of expulsion and allowing all exiled Palestinians, including the four expelled to Lebanon on January, 13, 1988, to return to their homes and families. Also the release of all administrative detainees and the cancellation of the hundreds of house arrest orders. In this connection, special mention must be made of the hundreds of applications for family reunions which we call upon the authorities to accept forthwith.

5. The immediate lifting of the siege of all Palestinian refugee camps in the West Bank and Gaza, and the withdrawal of the Israeli army from all population centers.

6. Carrying out a formal inquiry into the behavior of soldiers and settlers in the West Bank and Gaza, as well as inside jails and detention camps, and taking due punitive measures against all those convicted of having unduly caused death or bodily harm to unarmed civilians.

7. A cessation of all settlement activity and land confiscation and the release of lands already confiscated especially in the Gaza Strip. Also putting an end to the harassments and provocations of the Arab population by settlers in the West Bank and Gaza as well as in the Old City of Jerusalem. In particular, the curtailment of the provocative activities in the Old City of Jerusalem by Ariel Sharon and the ultra-religious settlers of Shuvu Banim and Ateret Kohanim.

8. Refraining from any act which might impinge on the Moslem and Christian holy sites or which might introduce changes to the status quo in the City of Jerusalem.

9. The cancellation of the Value Added Tax (V.A.T.) and all other direct Israeli taxes which are imposed on Palestinian residents in Jerusalem, the rest of the West Bank, and in Gaza; and putting an end to the harassment caused to Palestinian business and tradesmen.

10. The cancellation of all restrictions on political freedoms including restrictions on freedom of assembly and association; also making provisions for free municipal elections under the supervision of a neutral authority.

11. The immediate release of all funds deducted from the wages of laborers from the territories who worked and still work inside the

Green Line, which amount to several hundreds of millions of dollars. These accumulated deductions, with interest, must be returned to their rightful owners through the agency of the nationalist institutions headed by the Workers' Unions.

12. The removal of all restrictions on building permits and licences for industrial projects and artesian water wells as well as agricultural development programs in the occupied territories. Also rescinding all measures taken to deprive the territories of their water resources.

13. Terminating the policy of discrimination being practiced against industrial and agricultural produce from the occupied territories either by removing the restrictions on the transfer of goods to within the Green Line, or by placing comparable trade restrictions on the transfer of Israeli goods into the territories.

14. Removing the restrictions on political contacts between inhabitants of the occupied territories and the PLO, in such a way as to allow for the participation of Palestinians from the territories in the proceedings of the Palestine National Council, in order to ensure a direct input into the decision-making processes of the Palestinian nation by the Palestinians under occupation.

Palestinian nationalist   Jerusalem
institutions and personalities   January 14, 1988
from the West Bank and Gaza

APPENDIX XIV
THE SHULTZ INITIATIVE[8]
March 4, 1988

I set forth below the statement of understandings which I am convinced is necessary to achieve the prompt opening of negotiations on a comprehensive peace. This statement of understandings emerges from discussions held with you and other regional leaders. I look forward to the letter of reply of the Government of Israel in confirmation of this statement.

The agreed objective is a comprehensive peace providing for the security of all the states in the region and for the legitimate rights of the Palestinian people.

Negotiations will start on an early date certain between Israel and each of its neighbors which is willing to do so. These negotiations could begin by May 1, 1988. Each of these negotiations will be based on the

[8]Text of the letter that Secretary of State George P. Shultz wrote to Prime Minister Yitzhak Shamir of Israel outlining the American peace proposal. A similar letter was sent to King Hussein of Jordan. See *The New York Times*, March 10, 1988.

United Nations Security Council Resolutions 242 and 338, in all their parts. The parties to each bilateral negotiation will determine the procedure and agenda at their negotiation. All participants in the negotiations must state their willingness to negotiate with one another.

As concerns negotiations between the Israeli delegation and the Jordanian-Palestinian delegation, negotiations will begin on arrangements for a transitional period, with the objective of completing them within six months. Seven months after transitional negotiations begin, final status negotiations will begin, with the objective of completing them within one year. These negotiations will be based on all the provisions and principles of United Nations Security Council Resolution 242. Final status talks will start before the transitional period begins. The transitional period will begin three months after the conclusion of the transitional agreement and will last for three years. The United States will participate in both Negotiations and will promote their rapid conclusion. In particular, the United States will submit a draft agreement for the parties' consideration at the outset of the negotiations on transitional arrangements.

Two weeks before the opening of negotiations, an international conference will be held. The Secretary General of the United Nations will be asked to issue invitations to the parties involved in the Arab-Israeli conflict and the five permanent members of the United Nations Security Council. All participants in the conference must accept United Nations Security Council Resolutions 242 and 338, and renounce violence and terrorism. The parties to each bilateral negotiation may refer reports on the status of their negotiations to the conference, in a manner to be agreed. The conference will not be able to impose solutions or veto agreements reached.

Palestinian representation will be within the Jordanian-Palestinian delegation. The Palestinian issue will be addressed in the negotiations between the Jordanian-Palestinian and Israeli delegations. Negotiations between the Israeli delegation and the Jordanian-Palestinian delegation will proceed independently of any other negotiations.

This statement of understanding is an integral whole. The United States understands that your acceptance is dependent on the implementation of each element in good faith.

Sincerely yours,

George P. Shultz

<u>**APPENDIX XV**</u>
ISRAELI GOVERNMENT PEACE INITIATIVE
May 14, 1989

GENERAL:

1. This document presents the principles of a political initiative of the government of Israel which deals with the continuation of the peace process; the termination of the state of war with the Arab states; a solution for the Judea, Samaria and the Gaza District; peace with Jordan; and a resolution of the problem of the residents of the refugee camps in Judea, Samaria and the Gaza District.

2. The document includes:

A. The principles upon which the initiative is based.

B. Details of the processes for its implementation.

C. Reference to the subject of the elections under consideration. Further details relating to the elections as well as other objects of the initiative will be dealt with separately.

BASIC PREMISES:

3. The initiative is founded upon the assumption that there is a national consensus for it on the basis of the basic guidelines of the government of Israel, including the following points:

A. Israel yearns for peace and the continuation of the political process by means of direct negotiations based on the principles of the Camp David Accords.

B. Israel opposes the establishment of an additional Palestinian state in the Gaza District and in the area between Israel and Jordan.

C. Israel will not conduct negotiations with the PLO.

D. There will be no change in the status of Judea, Samaria and Gaza other than in accordance with the basic guidelines of the government.

SUBJECTS TO BE DEALT WITH IN THE PEACE PROCESS:

4. A. Israel views as important that the peace between Israel and Egypt, based on the Camp David Accords, will serve as a cornerstone for enlarging the circle of peace in the region, and calls for a common endeavor for the strengthening of the peace and its extension, through continued consultation.

B. Israel calls for the establishment of peaceful relations between it and those Arab states which still maintain a state of war with it, for the purpose of promoting a comprehensive settlement for the Arab-Israel conflict, including recognition, direct negotiations, ending the boycott, diplomatic relations, cessation of hostile activity in international institutions or forums and regional and bilateral cooperation.

C. Israel calls for an international endeavor to resolve the problem of the residents of the Arab refugee camps in Judea, Samaria and the Gaza District in order to improve their living conditions and to rehabilitate them. Israel is prepared to be a partner in this endeavor.

D. In order to advance the political negotiation process leading to peace, Israel proposes free and democratic elections among the Palestinian Arab inhabitants of Judea, Samaria and the Gaza District in an atmosphere devoid of violence, threats and terror. In these elections a representation will be chosen to conduct negotiations for a transitional period of self-rule. This period will constitute a test for coexistence and cooperation. At a later stage, negotiations will be conducted for a permanent solution, during which all the proposed options for an agreed settlement will be examined, and peace between Israel and Jordan will be achieved.

E. All above mentioned steps should be dealt with simultaneously.

F. The details of what has been mentioned in (D) above will be given below.

THE PRINCIPLES CONSTITUTING THE INITIATIVE STAGES:

5. The initiative is based on two stages:

A. Stage A—a transitional period for an interim agreement.

B. Stage B—permanent solution.

6. The interlock between the stages is a timetable on which the plan is built; the peace process delineated by the initiative is based on resolutions 242 and 338, upon which the Camp David Accords are founded.

Timetable:

7. The transitional period will continue for five years.

8. As soon as possible, but not later than the third year after the beginning of the transitional period, negotiations for achieving a permanent solution will begin.

Parties Participating in the Negotiations in Both Stages:

9. The parties participating in the negotiations for the first stage (the interim agreement) shall include Israel and the elected representation of the Palestinian Arab inhabitants of Judea, Samaria and the Gaza District. Jordan and Egypt will be invited to participate in these negotiations if they so desire.

10. The parties participating in the negotiations for the second stage (permanent solution) shall include Israel and the elected representation of the Palestinian Arab inhabitants of Judea, Samaria and the Gaza District, as well as Jordan; furthermore, Egypt may participate in these negotiations. In negotiations between Israel and Jordan, in which the elected representation of the Palestinian Arab inhabitants of Judea, Samaria and the Gaza District will participate, the peace treaty between Israel and Jordan will be concluded.

Substance of the transitional period:

11. During the transitional period the Palestinian Arab inhabitants of Judea, Samaria and the Gaza District will be accorded self-rule, by means of which they will, themselves, conduct their affairs of daily life. Israel will continue to be responsible for security, foreign affairs and all matters concerning Israeli citizens in Judea, Samaria and the Gaza District. Topics involving the implementation of the plan for self-rule will be considered and decided within the framework of the negotiations for an interim agreement.

Substance of the permanent solution:

12. In the negotiations for a permanent solution, every party shall be entitled to present for discussion all the subjects it may wish to raise.

13. The arrangements for peace and borders between Israel and Jordan.

DETAILS OF THE PROCESS FOR THE IMPLEMENTATION OF THE INITIATIVE

14. First and foremost, dialogue and basic agreement by the Palestinian Arab inhabitants of Judea, Samaria and the Gaza District, as well as Egypt and Jordan if they wish to take part, as above mentioned, in the negotiations on the principles constituting the initiative.

15. A. Immediately afterwards will follow the stage of preparations and implementation of the election process in which a

representation of the Palestinian Arab inhabitants of Judea, Samaria and Gaza will be elected.

This representation:

I. Shall be a partner to the conduct of negotiations for the transitional period (interim agreement).

II. Shall constitute the self-governing authority in the course of the transitional period.

III. Shall be the central Palestinian component, subject to agreement after three years, in the negotiations for the permanent solution.

B. In the period of the preparations and implementation there shall be a calming of the violence in Judea, Samaria and the Gaza District.

16. As to the substance of the elections, it is recommended that a proposal of regional elections be adopted, the details of which shall be determined in further discussions.

17. Every Palestinian Arab residing in Judea, Samaria and the Gaza District, who shall be elected by the inhabitants to represent them—after having submitted his candidacy in accordance with the detailed document which shall determine the subject of the elections—may be a legitimate participant in the conduct of negotiations with Israel.

18. The elections shall be free, democratic and secret.

19. Immediately after the election of the Palestinian representation, negotiations shall be conducted with it on an interim agreement for a transitional period which shall continue for five years, as mentioned above. In these negotiations, the parties shall determine all the subjects relating to the substance of the self-rule and the arrangements necessary for its implementation.

20. As soon as possible, but not later than the third year after the establishment of the self-rule, negotiations for a permanent solution shall begin. During the whole period of these negotiations until the signing of the agreement for a permanent solution, the self-rule shall continue in effect as determined in the negotiations for an interim agreement.

APPENDIX XVI
EXCERPT FROM
SECRETARY OF STATE JAMES A. BAKER III'S TESTIMONY
ON THE PEACE PROCESS[9]
May 22, 1991

First, general agreement that the objective of the process is a comprehensive settlement achieved through direct negotiations based on UN Security Council Resolutions 242 and 338.

Second, broad understanding that the negotiating process would proceed simultaneously along two tracks, involving direct negotiations between Israel and Arab states and between Israel and Palestinians from the Occupied Territories.

Third, agreement that the negotiations between Israel and Palestinians would proceed in phases, with talks on interim self-government preceding negotiations over the permanent status of the Occupied Territories.

Fourth, agreement that Palestinians would be represented in the process by leaders from the Occupied Territories who accept the two-track process and phased approach to negotiations and who commit to living in peace with Israel.

Fifth, general acceptance that a conference, co-sponsored by the United States and the Soviet Union, would break the old taboos about public contacts between the parties and be the launching pad for direct negotiations between the parties.

APPENDIX XVII
SELECTED PALESTINIAN QUOTES

Statement by the PLO Executive Committee on the Camp David Agreements, issued in Beirut, September 18, 1978:
    The Camp David meeting has resulted in an agreement which is the most dangerous link in the chain of the hostile conspiracy that has been in progress since 1948. It represents what Zionism and American imperialism have been seeking to achieve for thirty years. . .
The Palestinian revolution warns all suspect quarters that try to build a place for themselves in the self-government conspiracy and declare their support for the Camp David conspiracy that they will have to face the will of our people and their just penalty. . . (Issued by the Palestinian news agency *Wafa* on September 18, 1978.)

---

[9] Secretary of State James A. Baker's testimony before the House Appropriations Subcommittee on Foreign Operations.

<u>Statement by the West Bank National Conference which met in Beit Hanina, Jerusalem, October 1, 1978:</u>
  8. We reject the self-government plan both in its form and content. It is a plan to consolidate the occupation, to continue the oppression of our people and the usurping of our legitimate rights. It is an open ploy to bypass the ambitions of our people and our right to our own self-determination. . . . (Published in the PLO weekly *Filastin al-Thawra*, Beirut, October 9, 1978.)

<u>Resolutions passed at the Gaza National Conference which met at Gaza, October 16 and 18, 1978:</u>
  8. Self-government according to the Camp David agreement is without content or meaning since it does not fulfill even the minimum demands and rights of the Palestinian Arab people nor does it represent the correct manner in which that people can exercise their right to freedom and self-determination. This is because it is obscure, ambiguous and complex and lacks specific genuine guarantees which ensure for that people their freedom, their return and self-determination on their soil and in their homeland. (Published in the Arabic-language newspaper of the Israeli Communist Party (Rakah), *al-Ittihad*, Haifa, October 24, 1978.)

The Camp David Agreement and the Palestine Problem:
  D. If the Camp David process gets off the ground and is permitted to reach its ordained destination, the most that it can offer the Palestinian people will be the following:
  A fraction of the Palestinian people (under one-third of the whole) may attain a fraction of its rights (not including its inalienable right to self-determination and statehood) in a fraction of its homeland (less than one-fifth of the area of the whole).
  This promise is to be fulfilled several years from now, through a step-by-step process in which Israel is able at every point to exercise a decisive veto power over any agreement.
  Beyond that, the vast majority of Palestinians is condemned to permanent loss of its Palestinian national identity, to permanent exile, to the permanent separation of most Palestinians from one another and from Palestine—in short, to a life without national hope or meaning. (Sayegh, Fayez A., *Journal of Palestine Studies*, Winter 1979, Vol. VIII, No. 2, p. 40.)

<u>The Mayor of Gaza, Rashad Shawa:</u>
  They will tell the world that they have given self-rule, autonomy, to the people of the occupied territories, starting with Gaza, when in fact the whole thing will be fictitious: The Palestinians who are now in office will still be unable to take any decision, and if they run into any difficulty in the course of their duties, they will still have to refer to their seniors—who will not be Arab ministers, but Israeli rulers . . . (Beirut weekly *Monday Morning* January 21, 1980 quoted in *Journal of Palestine Studies*, Spring 1980, Vol IX. No. 3, pp. 179-180.)

The Mayor of Halhul, Muhammad Milhem:
Autonomy in the political context means a certain status for a minority within a state. Thus, it does not lead to statehood for the minority. Autonomy cannot lead us to an independent Palestinian state. (Interview in *Journal of Palestine Studies*, Autumn 1979, Vol. IX, No. 1, p. 114.)

Naseer H. Aruri and Fouad M. Moughrabi:
All these qualifications of "self-government"—with regard to water, public security, and Israeli security; the fact that this concept is to be ultimately defined only during the negotiations; and the stipulation that self-government in the West Bank and Gaza must be exercised "in association with Jordan,"—lead inevitably to the conclusion that the Reagan plan conforms more with the concept of a limited autonomy than with the "full" autonomy promised at Camp David. (*Journal of Palestine Studies*, Winter 1983, Vol. XII, No. 2, p. 23.)

Faisal Husayni:
Look, even for the elections, if they were part of a package deal, if they would be the first in a series of steps at the end of which we would have our state, it would be another story. (*Journal of Palestine Studies*, Summer 1989,Vol. XVIII, No. 4, p. 14.)

Walid Khalidi:
There is no quarrel with the concept of a transitional period leading to a final settlement. One cannot leap from the present situation to final settlement in one go. The concept of a transitional period was endorsed by the Arab heads of state as early as the 1982 Fez Summit.
The key issue in the concept of a transitional period is its function. What central purpose is the transitional period supposed to serve? According to Baker, the transitional period "will allow the parties to take the measure of each other's performance, to encourage attitudes to change and to demonstrate that peace and coexistence are desired."
If this indeed is the purpose of the transitional period, it is to be wondered how this could be achieved in the absence of a halt to Israeli settlement and the concomitant land seizure. (*Journal of Palestine Studies* Spring 1990, Vol. XIX, No. 3, p. 31).

Radi Jarra'i:
. . . To take a practical step, I propose that the Palestine National Council dissolve itself and allow itself to be restructured in a way to give the right number of seats for the Palestinians in the West Bank and Gaza Strip in accordance to the population. . . .
The second step would be to establish a transitional government or government in exile which would include members of the PNC from the West bank and Gaza Strip. Step three is for this government to supervise all national institutions in the West Bank and Gaza, such as those involved in health, society, education and religion.
Step four: To announce a willingness to negotiate with Israel based on UN resolutions so that peace will prevail in this region under

international supervision. The other party will have to negotiate with Jordan for the establishment of a confederacy after Palestinian independence. We also have to ask the international community, the United Nations and all peace-loving nations to support our program. (Jerusalem-based *al-Fajr*, April 1, 1991, p. 4.)

Talal Abu Afifeh (al-Safi):
The following are the main points of the peace program:
Stage One—elections—in the course of the first year, both sides, the Israeli and Palestinian, will make several good-will gestures which will help build up mutual trust. . . .
Stage Two—a temporary transitional stage lasting three years. Within one year the Israeli and Palestinian representative must agree upon "extended self-rule" authority for the Palestinians. The talks will be held in Cairo, under the supervision of observers from the United States, the Soviet Union, Egypt and the European Common Market (Troika). The Palestinian administrative government will establish ten ministries, including police and interior ministries, and will found a local police. At this stage, there will be a symbolical presence of international military forces in the Territories and the IDF will withdraw from the Arab settlements in the Territories. (*Arabs in Israel,* May 26, 1991).

Hanan Ashrawi:
As far as autonomy is concerned, I think—was it three or four years ago—at the beginning of *intifadah* we said autonomy is a defunct word. It no longer exists in our dictionary. (Laughs.) So I don't think anybody has used the term autonomy in any of the discussions we have had, whether it's Palestinians or American. (Federal News Service. Press Conference/The Latest Developments in the Middle East Peace Process. Moderator: Mr. Hasan Rahman, The Palestinian Affairs Center, National Press Club, Washington D.C., July 3, 1991.)

Haidar Abdelshafi:
We have already declared our acceptance of transitional phases as part of this process, provided they have the logic of internal coherence and interconnection, within a specified, limited time frame and without prejudicing the permanent status. During the transitional phase, Palestinians must have meaningful control over decisions affecting their lives and fate. During this phase, the immediate repatriation of the 1967 displaced persons and the reunion of separated families can be carried out. (*Mideast Mirror*, November 1, 1991, p.16)

RECENT PUBLICATIONS OF THE WASHINGTON INSTITUTE

Peace Process Briefing Book—An authoritative guide to the Arab-Israeli peace process with maps and documents.

GulfWatch Anthology—A collection of the day-by-day analyses of the Gulf crisis as it was analyzed by the scholars and associates of the Washington Institute.

American Strategy After the Gulf War—Proceedings of the Washington Institute's 1991 Soref Symposium with Secretary of Defense Richard Cheney and Israeli Knesset Member Ze'ev Binyamin Begin.

After the Storm: An American Strategy for the Postwar Middle East—The interim report of The Washington Institute's Strategic Study Group.

Restoring the Balance: U.S. Strategy and the Gulf Crisis—The initial report of The Washington Institute's Strategic Study Group.

Policy Paper 26: *Damascus Courts the West: Syrian Politics, 1989-1991* by Daniel Pipes

Policy Paper 25: *Economic Consequences of Peace for Israel, the Palestinians, and Jordan* by Patrick L. Clawson and Howard Rosen

Policy Paper 24: *The Future of Iraq* by Laurie Mylroie

Policy Paper 23: *"The Poor Man's Atomic Bomb?": Biological Weapons in the Middle East* by W. Seth Carus

Policy Focus 15: *Israel and the Gulf Crisis: Changing Security Requirements on the Eastern Front* by Dore Gold

Policy Focus 14: *Iraq's Economic and Military Vulnerabilities* by Patrick Clawson and W. Seth Carus

Policy Paper 21: *"The Sword of the Arabs:" Iraq's Strategic Weapons* by Michael Eisenstadt

Policy Paper 19: *In Through the Out Door: Jordan's Disengagement and the Peace Process* by Asher Susser

Policy Paper 15: *Security for Peace: Israel's Minimal Security Requirements in Negotiations with the Palestinians* by Ze'ev Schiff

Policy Paper 14: *The Genie Unleashed: Iraq's Chemical and Biological Weapons Program* by W. Seth Carus

For a complete listing or to order publications, write or call The Washington Institute for Near East Policy, 1828 L Street, NW, Suite 1050, Washington, D.C. 20036, Phone (202) 452-0650, Fax (202) 223-5364.